LUNARBABOON
The Daily Life of Parenthood

Thanks for
the support!

[signature]

LUNARBABOON
The Daily Life of Parenthood

Remember not having kids?
Not really.
SHH! Quiet you two!

Chris Grady

Andrews McMeel
PUBLISHING®

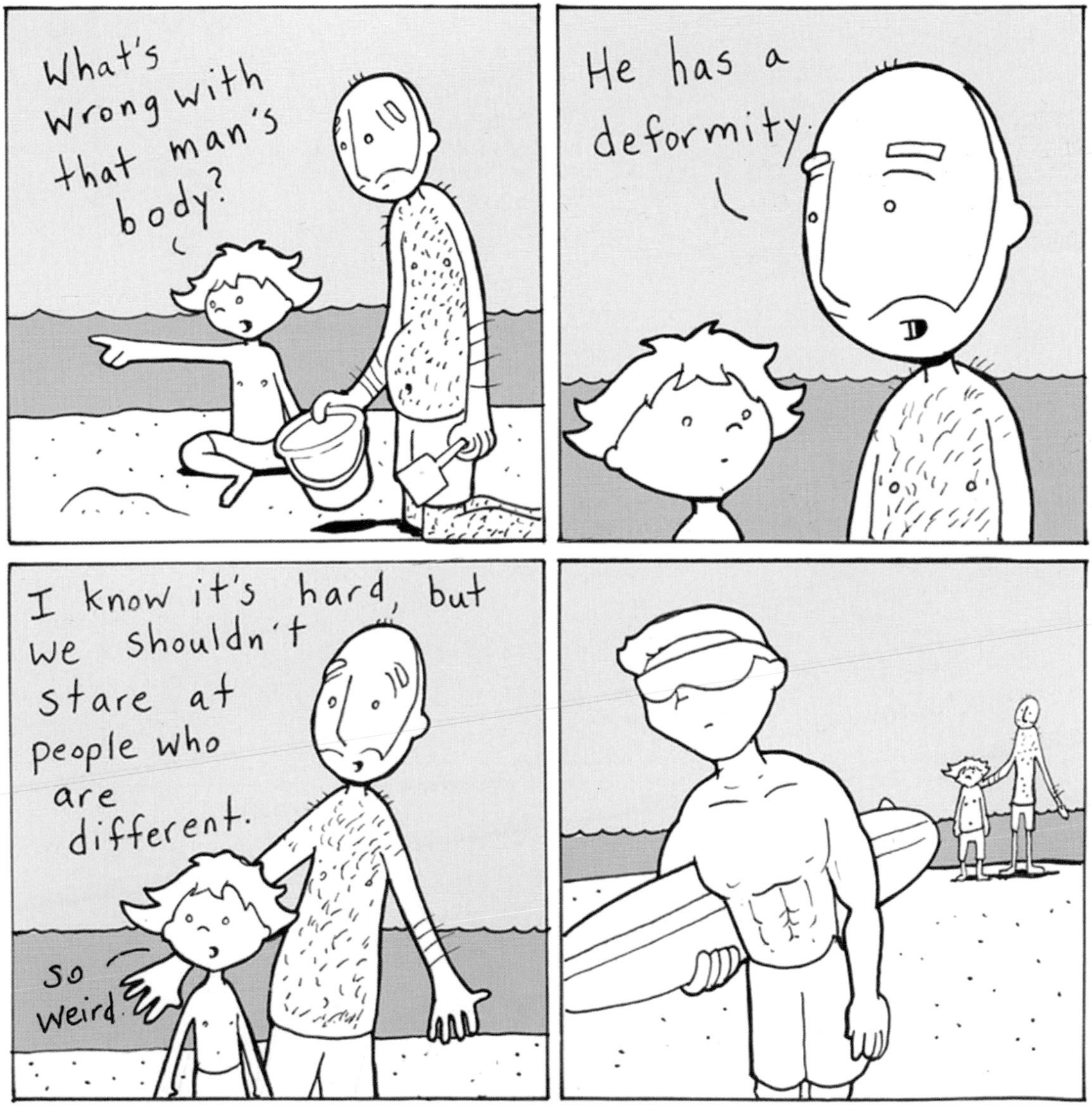
What's wrong with that man's body?
He has a deformity.
I know it's hard, but we shouldn't stare at people who are different.
So weird.

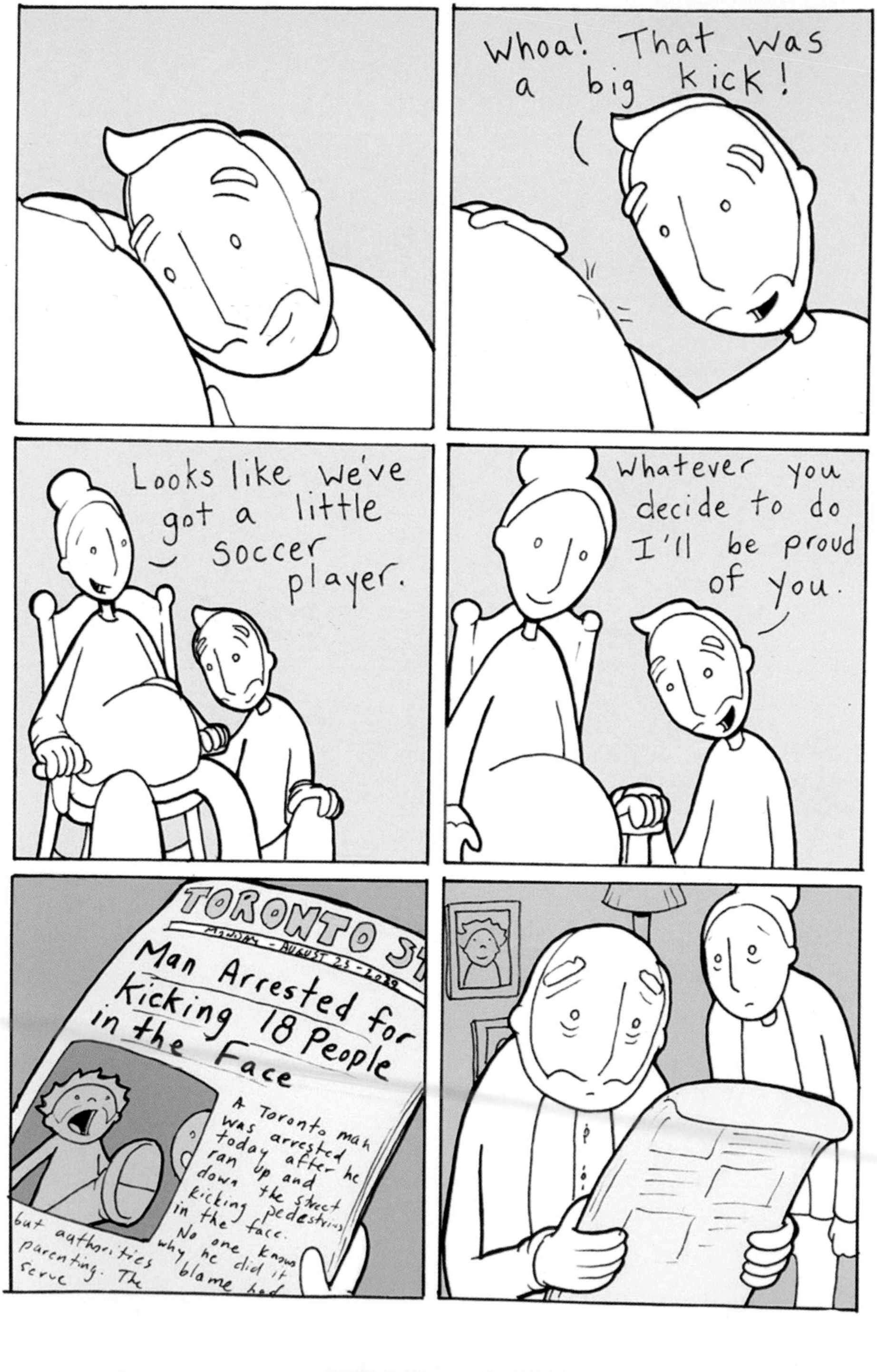
Whoa! That was a big kick!
Looks like we've got a little soccer player.
Whatever you decide to do I'll be proud of you.
TORONTO
Man Arrested for Kicking 18 People in the Face
A Toronto man was arrested today after he ran up and down the street kicking pedestrians in the face.
No one knows why he did it but authorities blame bad parenting. The
serve

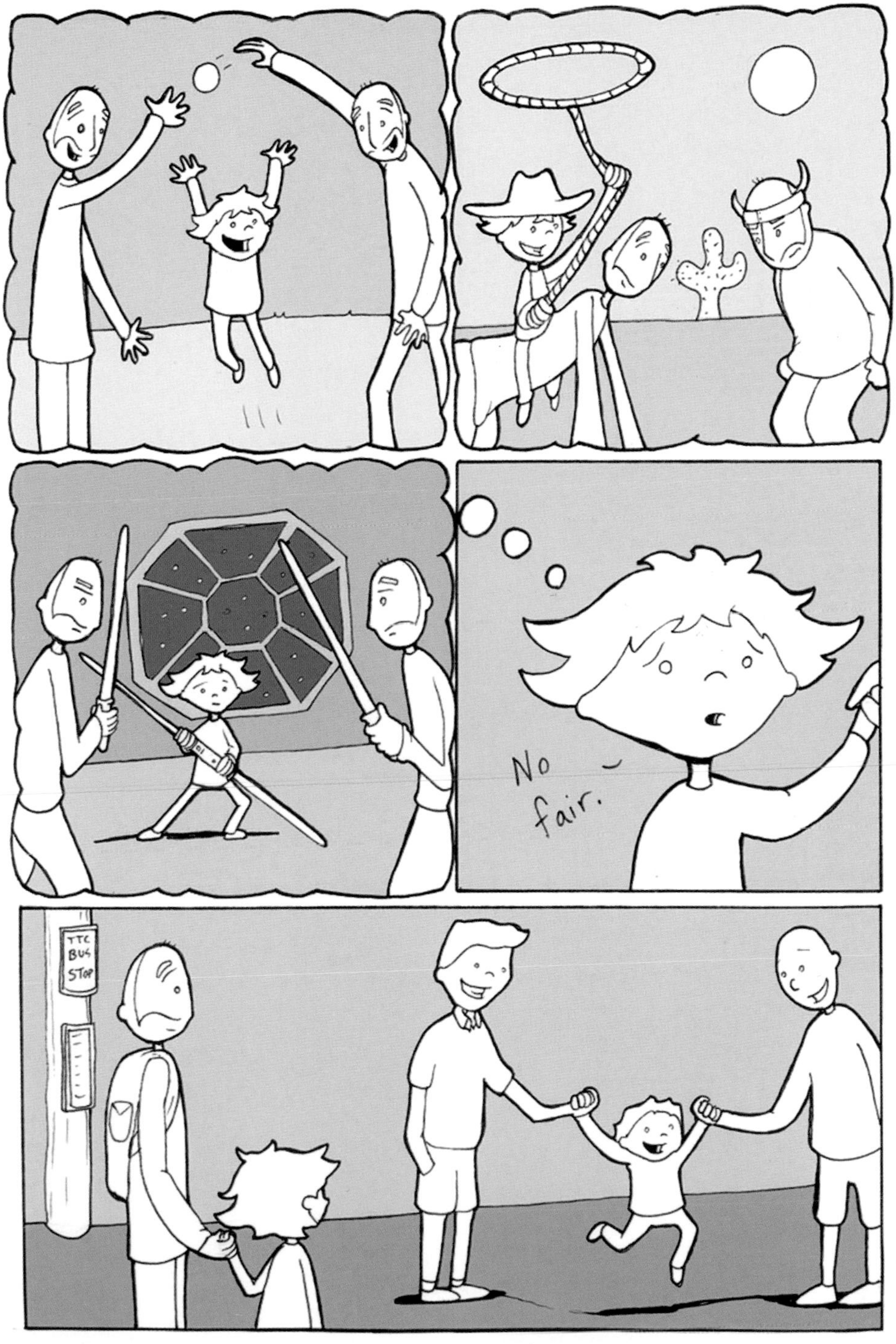
No – fair.
TTC BUS STOP

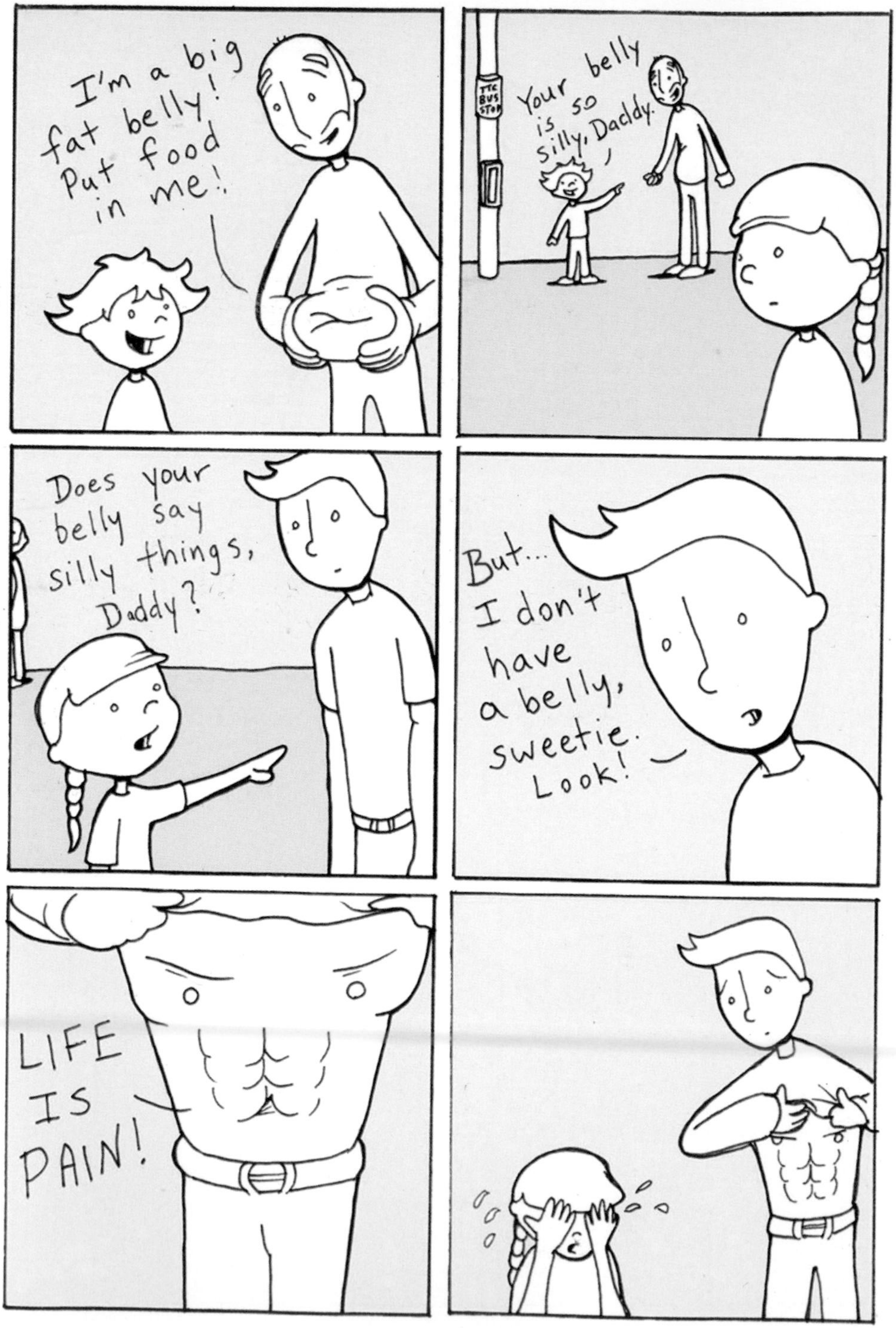
I'm a big fat belly! Put food in me!
TTC BUS STOP
Your belly is so silly, Daddy.
Does your belly say silly things, Daddy?
But... I don't have a belly, sweetie. Look!
LIFE IS PAIN!

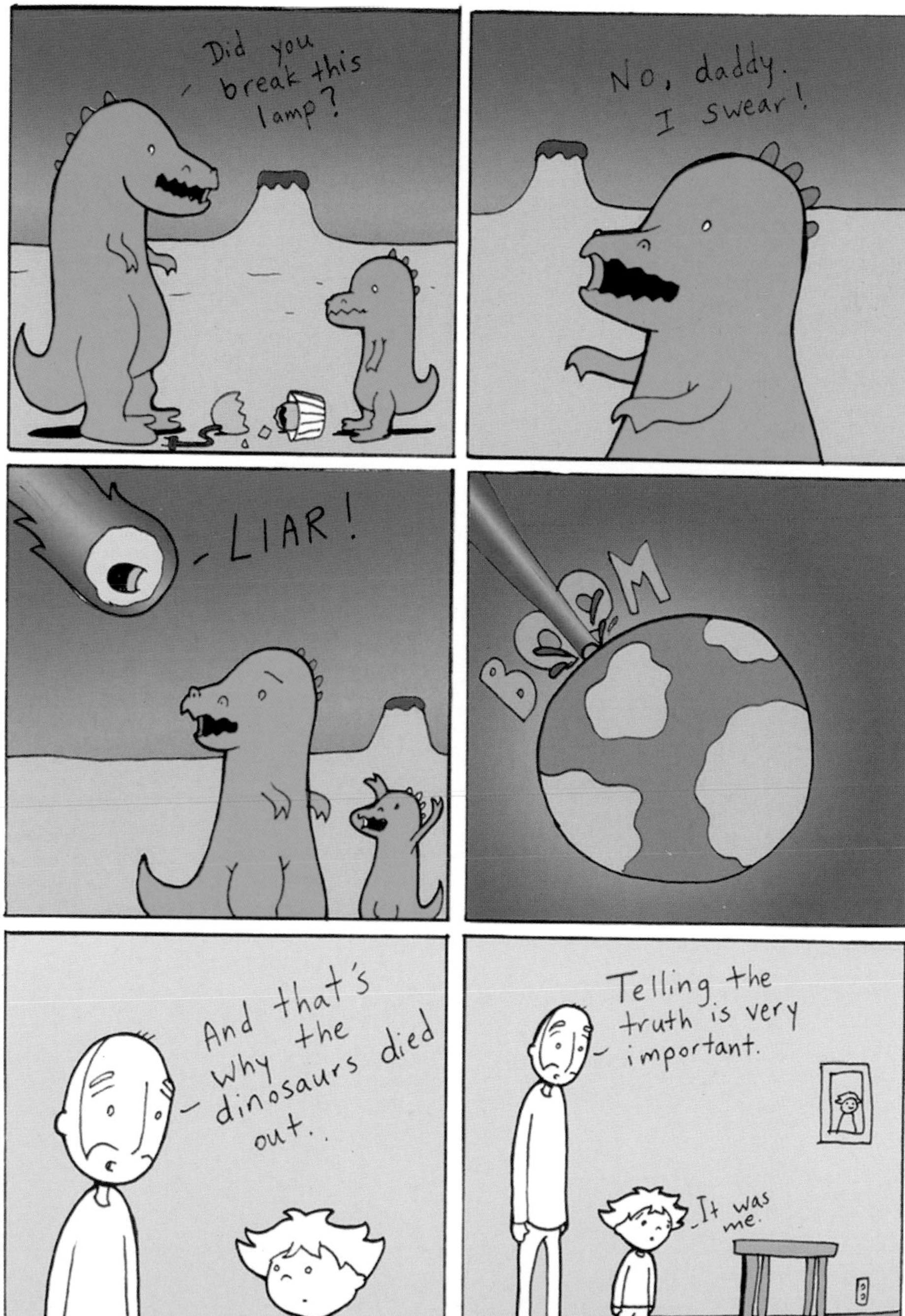
Did you break this lamp?
No, daddy. I swear!
LIAR!
BOOM
And that's why the dinosaurs died out.
Telling the truth is very important.
It was me.

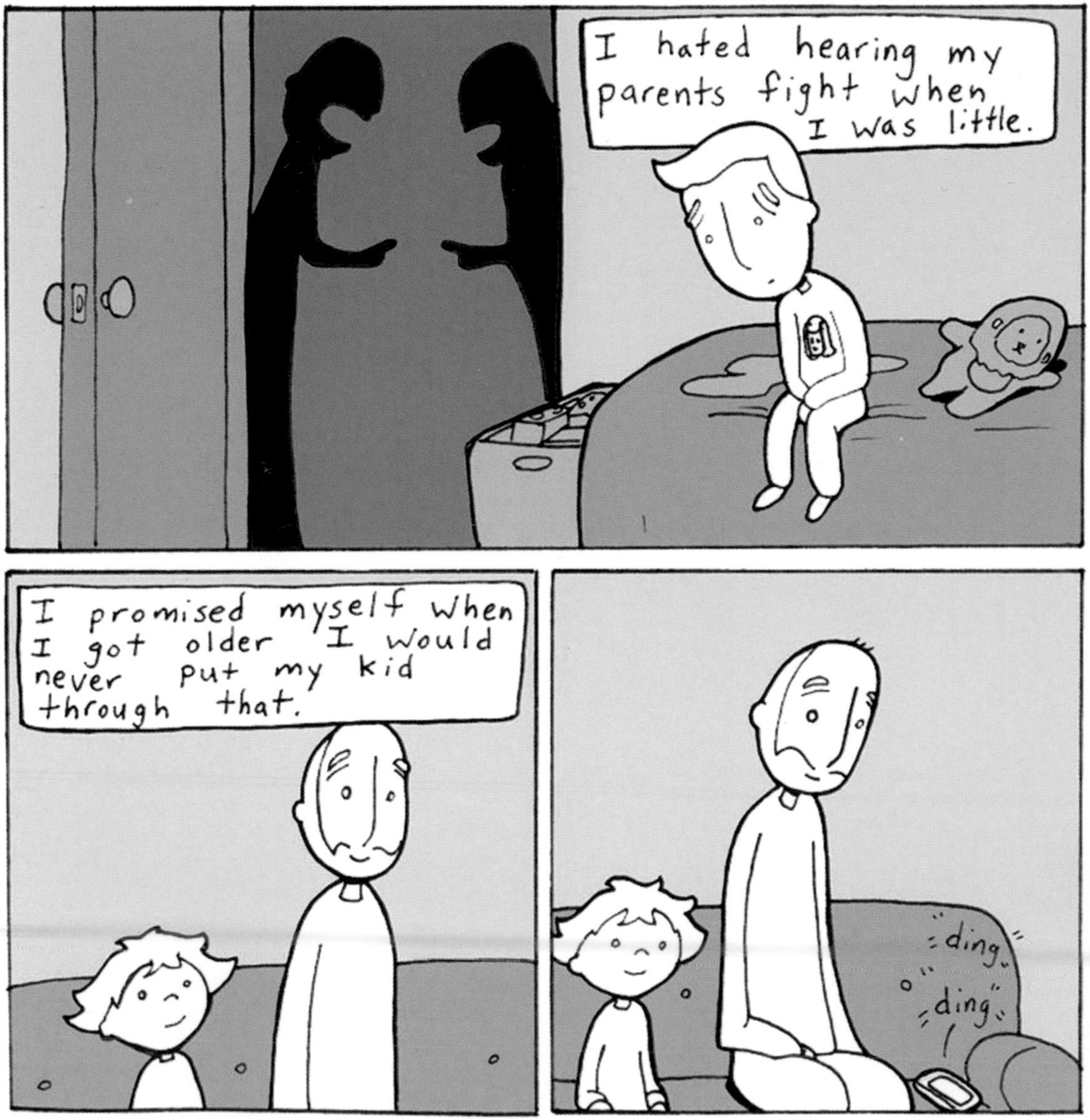
I hated hearing my parents fight when I was little.
I promised myself when I got older I would never put my kid through that.
ding
ding

WOULD YOU PLEASE CLEAN UP YOUR SHIT!?
I'M NOT YOUR MAID!
tap tap
tap
tap
"DING"
tap
tap
tap

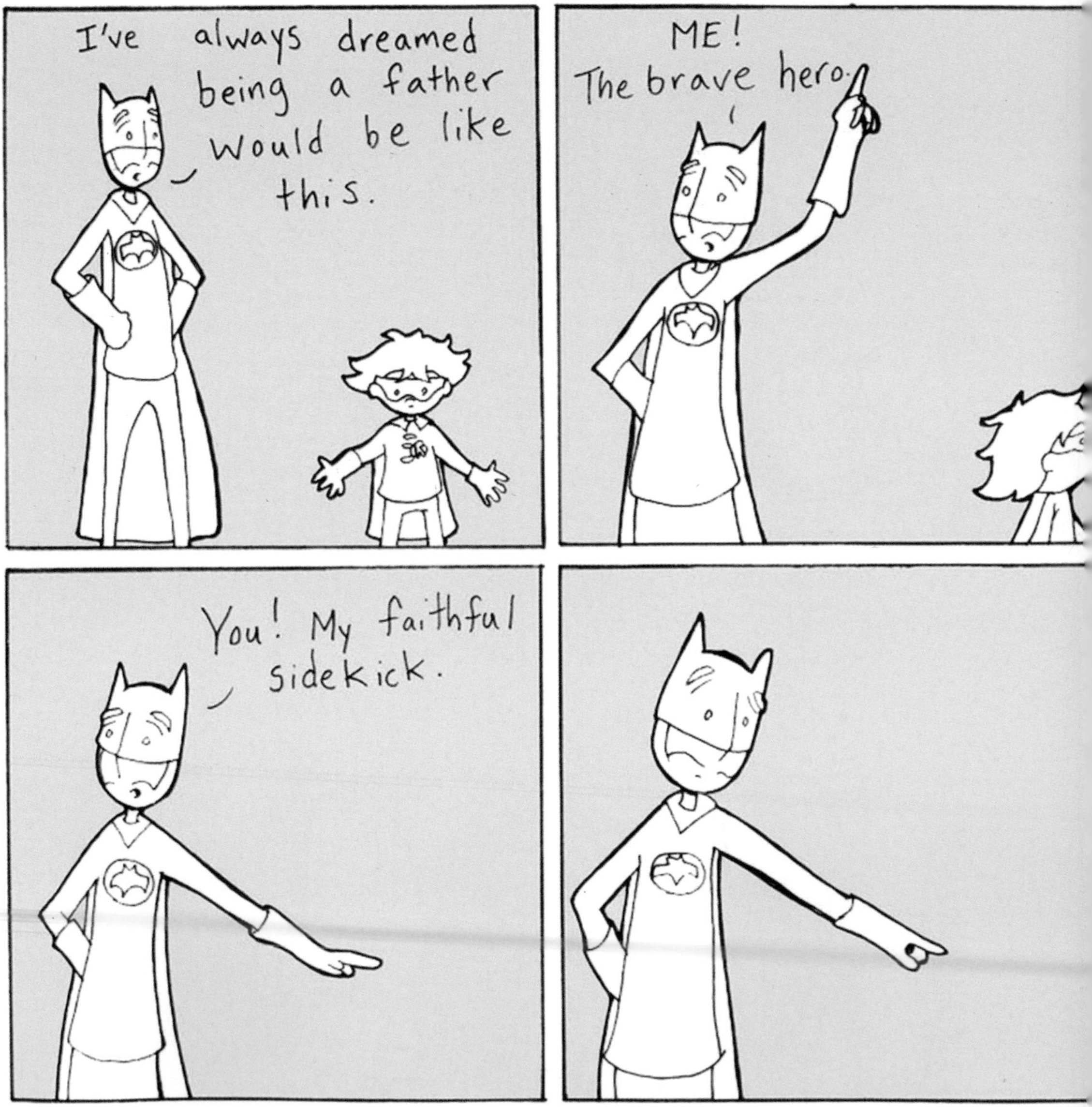
I've always dreamed being a father would be like this.
ME! The brave hero.
You! My faithful sidekick.

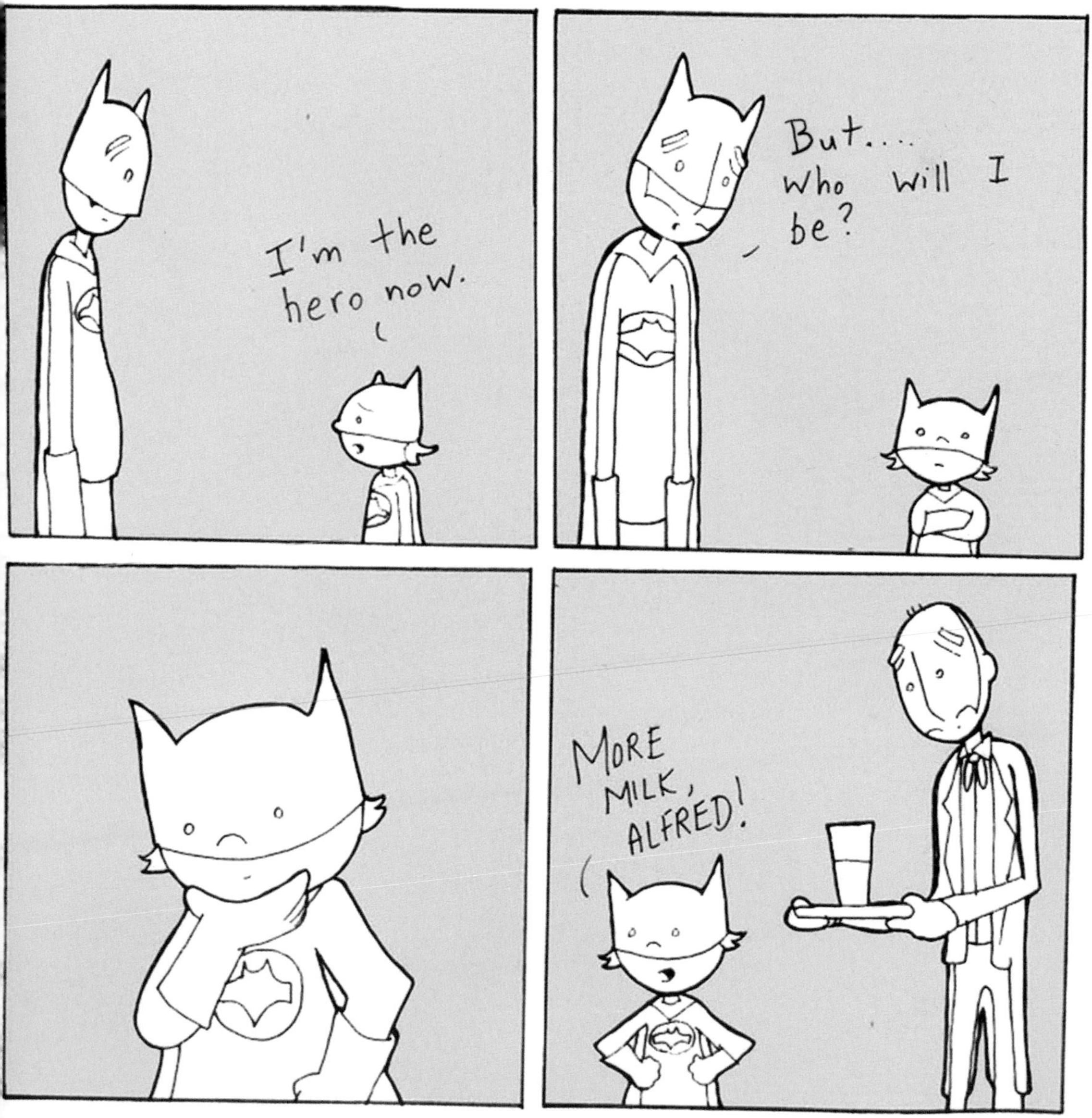
I'm the hero now.
But.... who will I be?
MORE MILK, ALFRED!

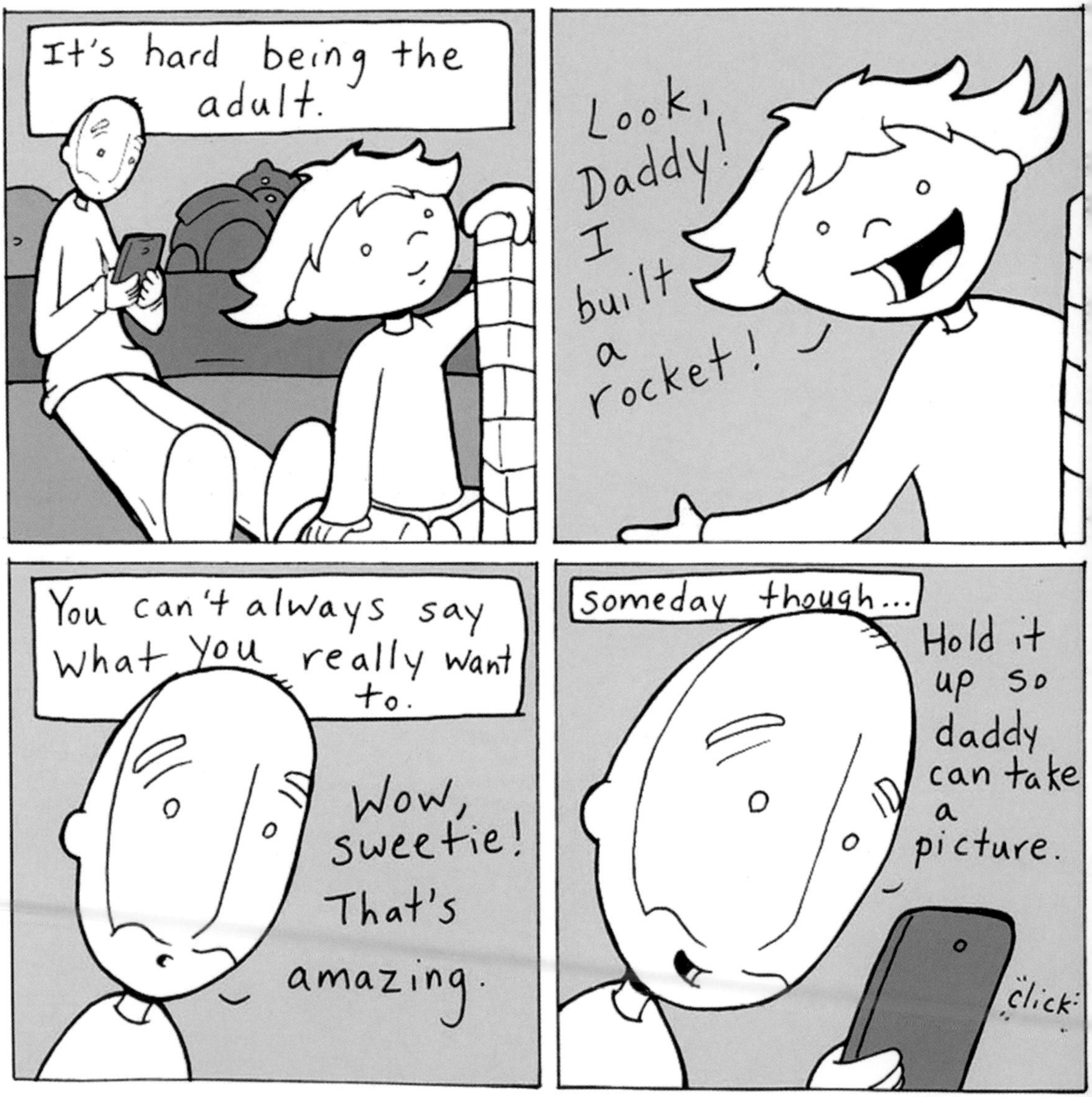
It's hard being the adult.
Look, Daddy! I built a rocket!
You can't always say what you really want to.
Wow, sweetie! That's amazing.
Someday though...
Hold it up so daddy can take a picture.
click

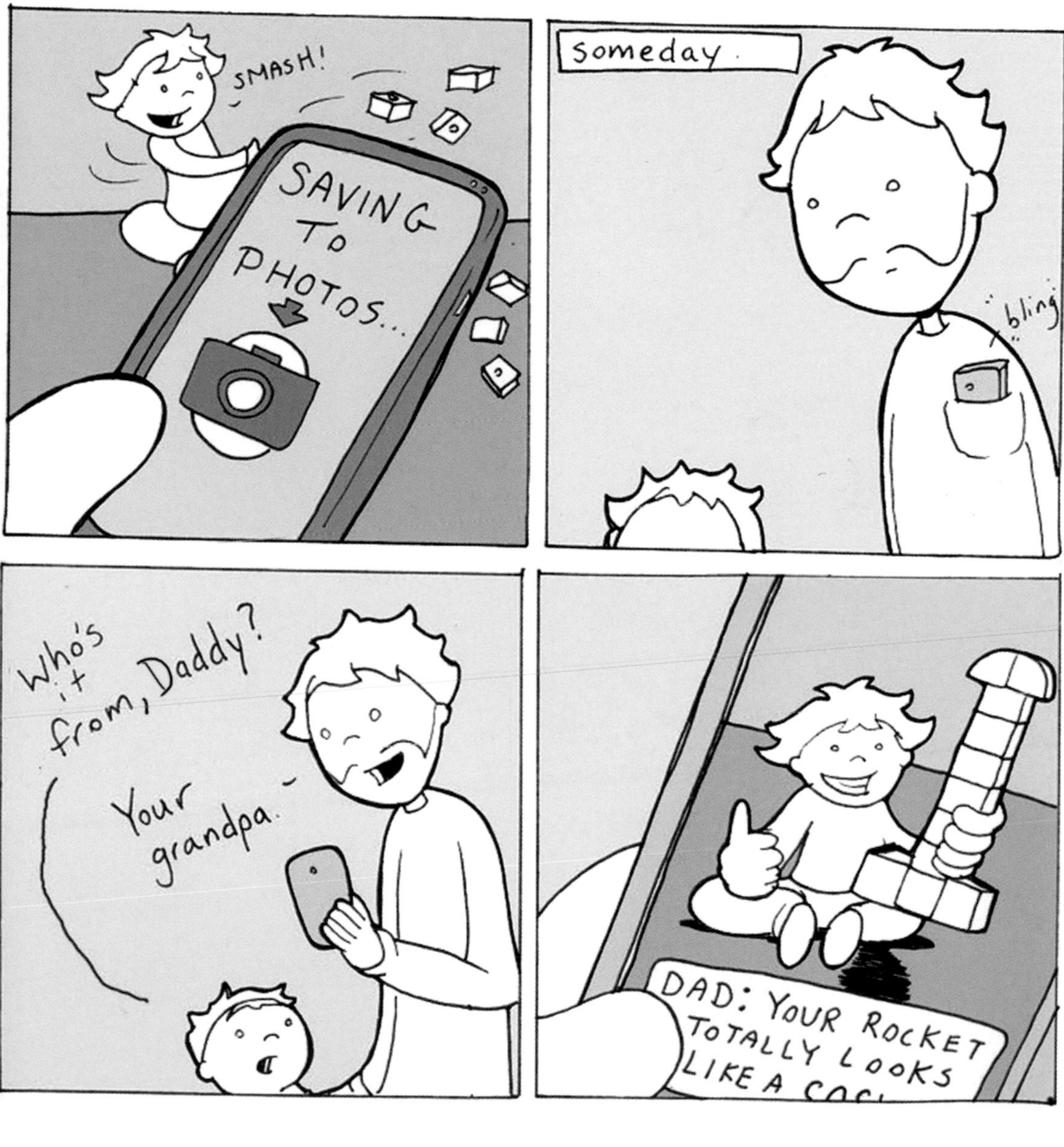
SMASH!
SAVING TO PHOTOS...
Someday.
bling
Who's it from, Daddy?
Your grandpa.
DAD: YOUR ROCKET TOTALLY LOOKS LIKE A

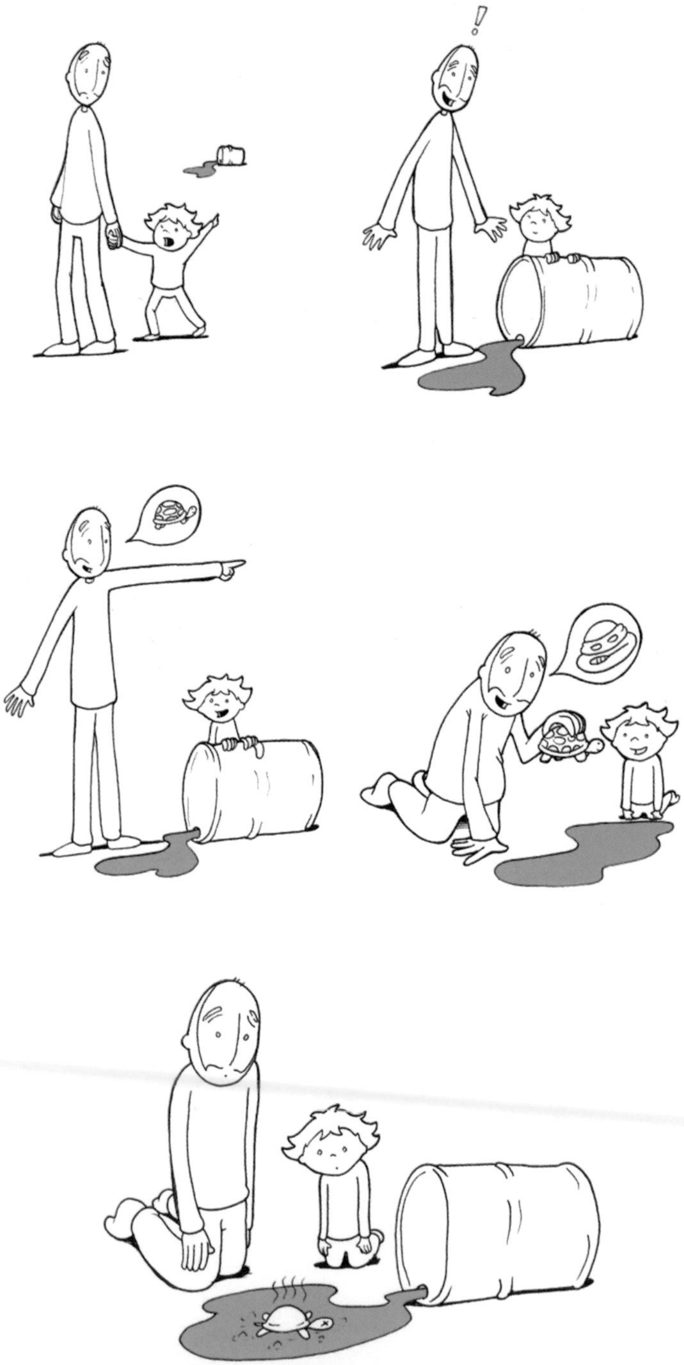
!

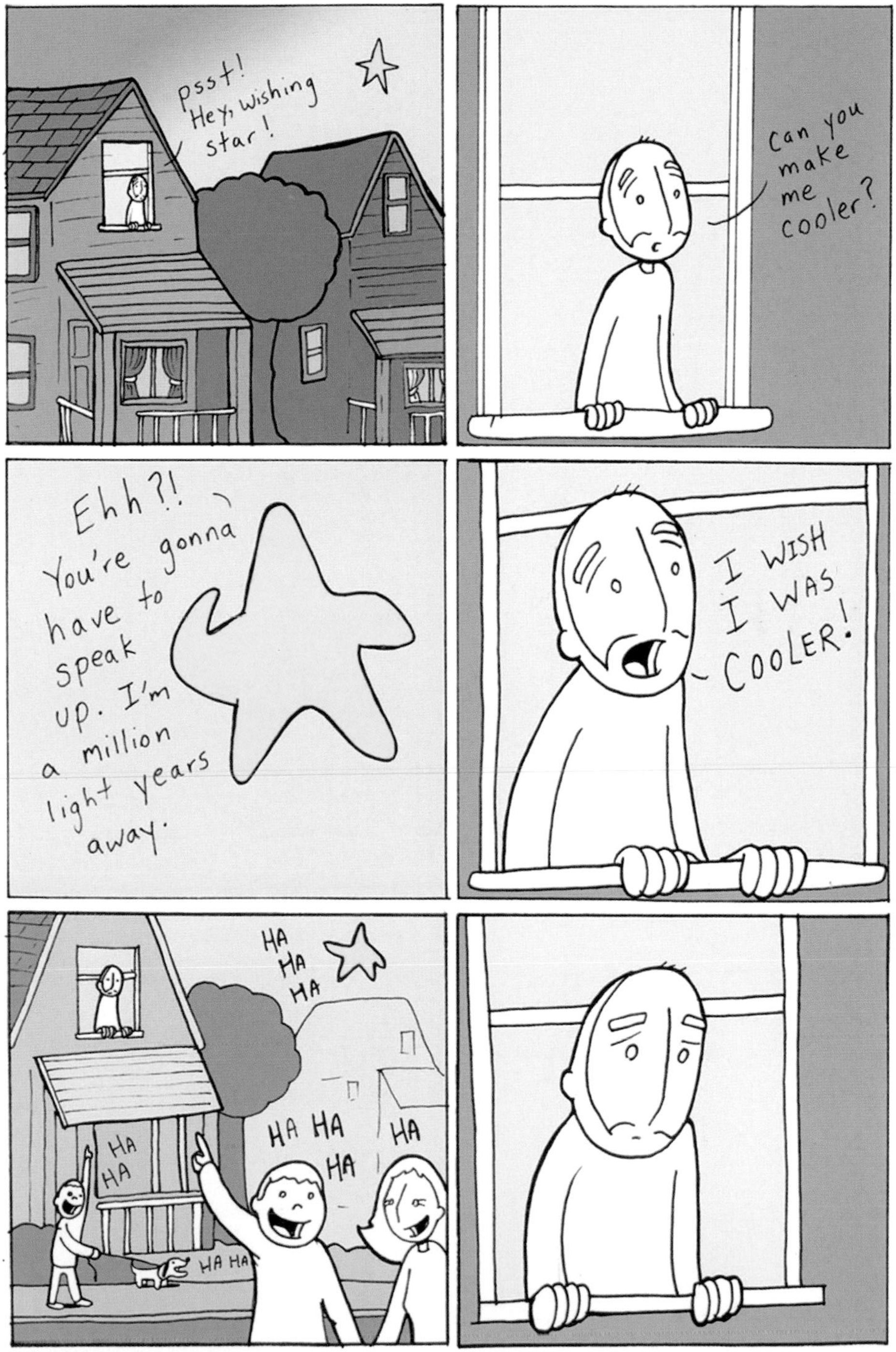
psst! Hey, wishing star!
Can you make me cooler?
Ehh?! You're gonna have to speak up. I'm a million light years away.
I WISH I WAS COOLER!
HA HA HA
HA HA
HA HA HA HA
HA HA

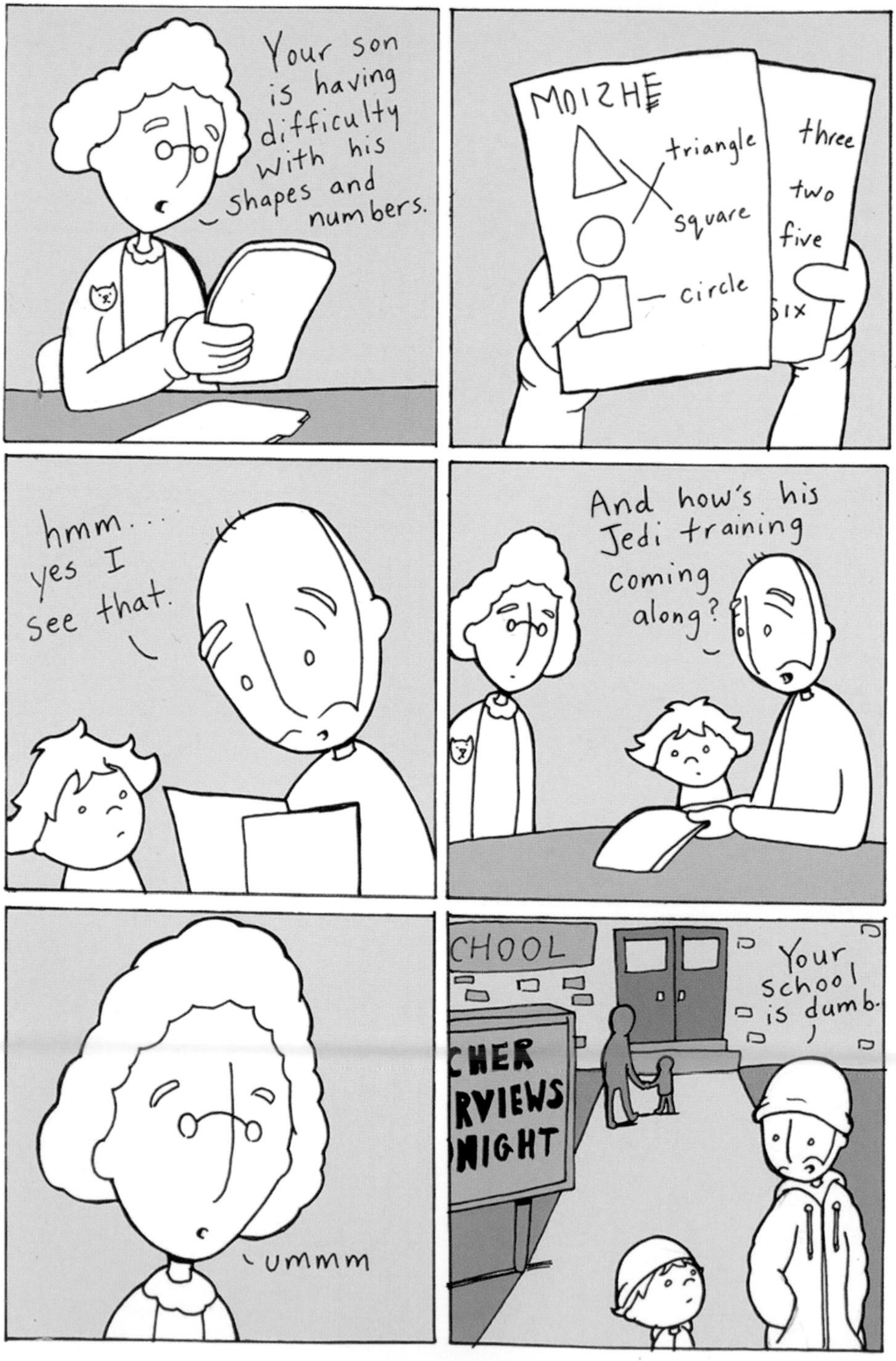
Your son is having difficulty with his shapes and numbers.
MOIZHE
triangle
square
circle
three
two
five
six
hmm... yes I see that.
And how's his Jedi training coming along?
ummm
CHOOL
CHER
RVIEWS
NIGHT
Your school is dumb.

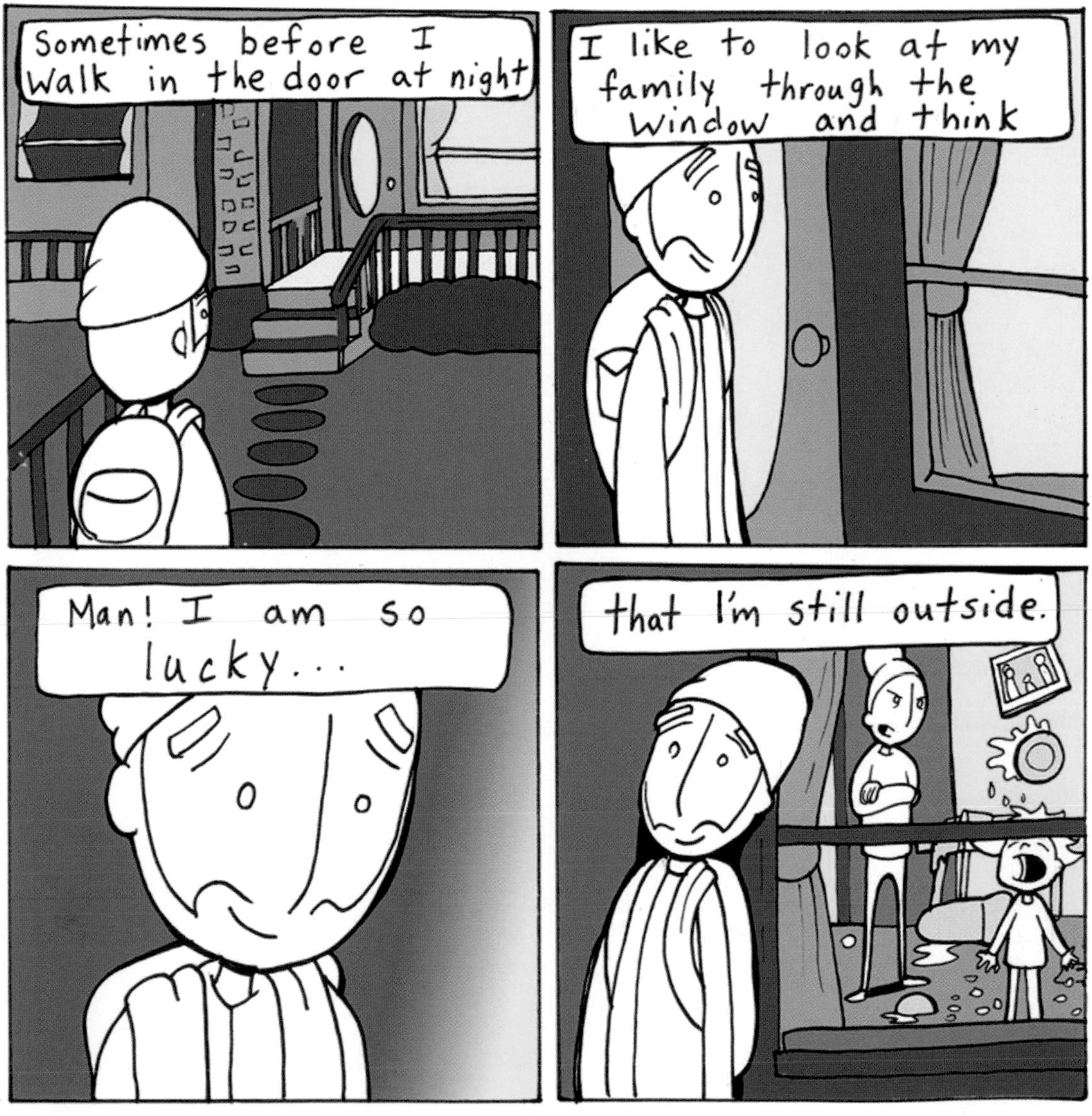
Sometimes before I walk in the door at night
I like to look at my family through the window and think
Man! I am so lucky...
that I'm still outside.

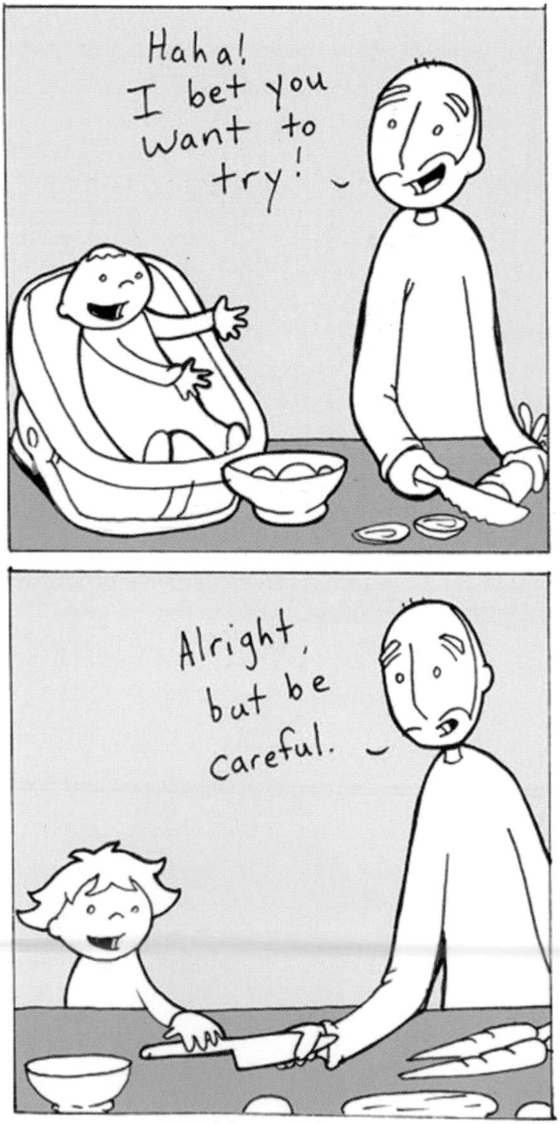
Haha! I bet you want to try!
You're not quite ready yet.
Alright, but be careful.
Almost got it.

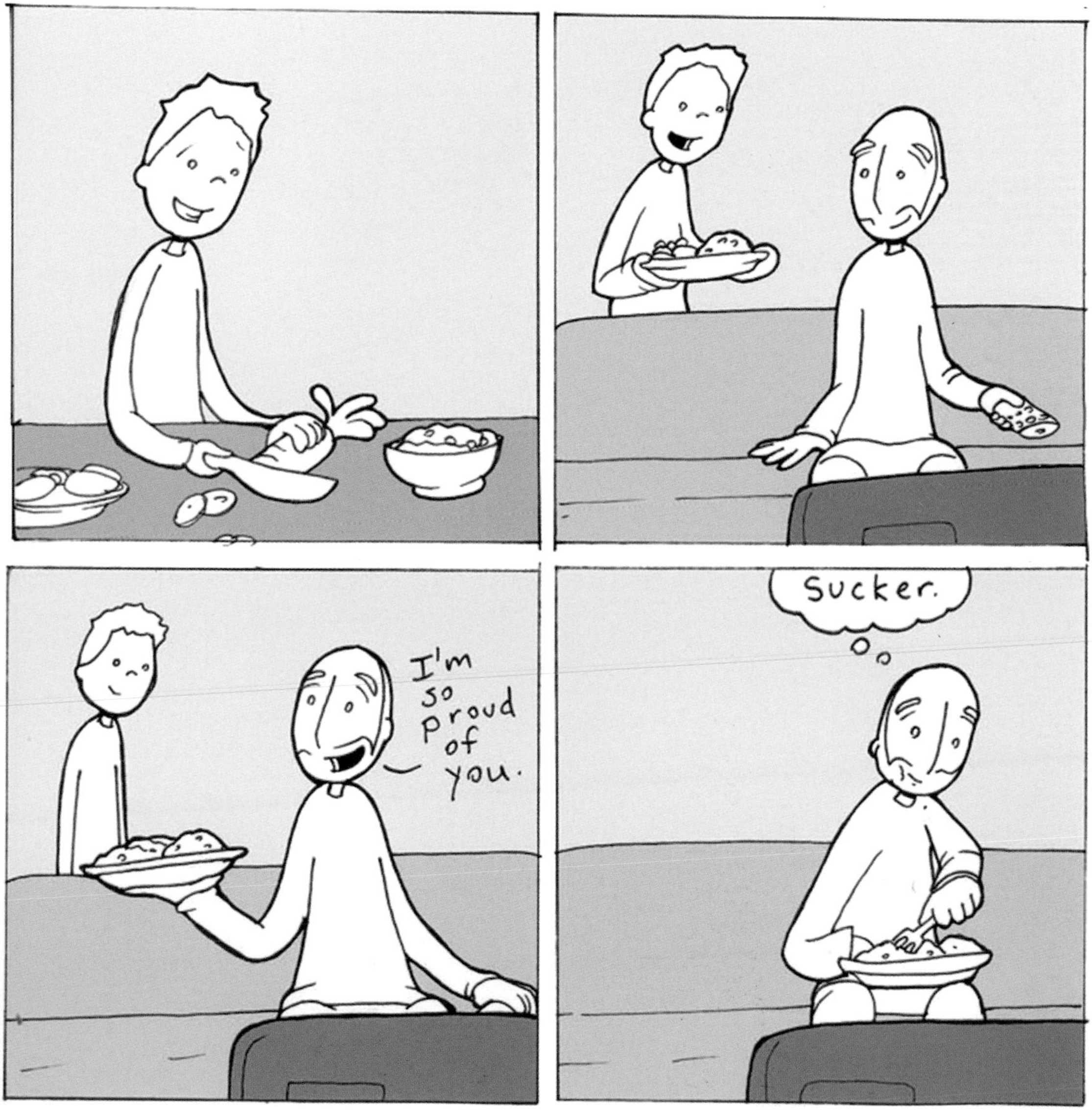
I'm so proud of you.
Sucker.

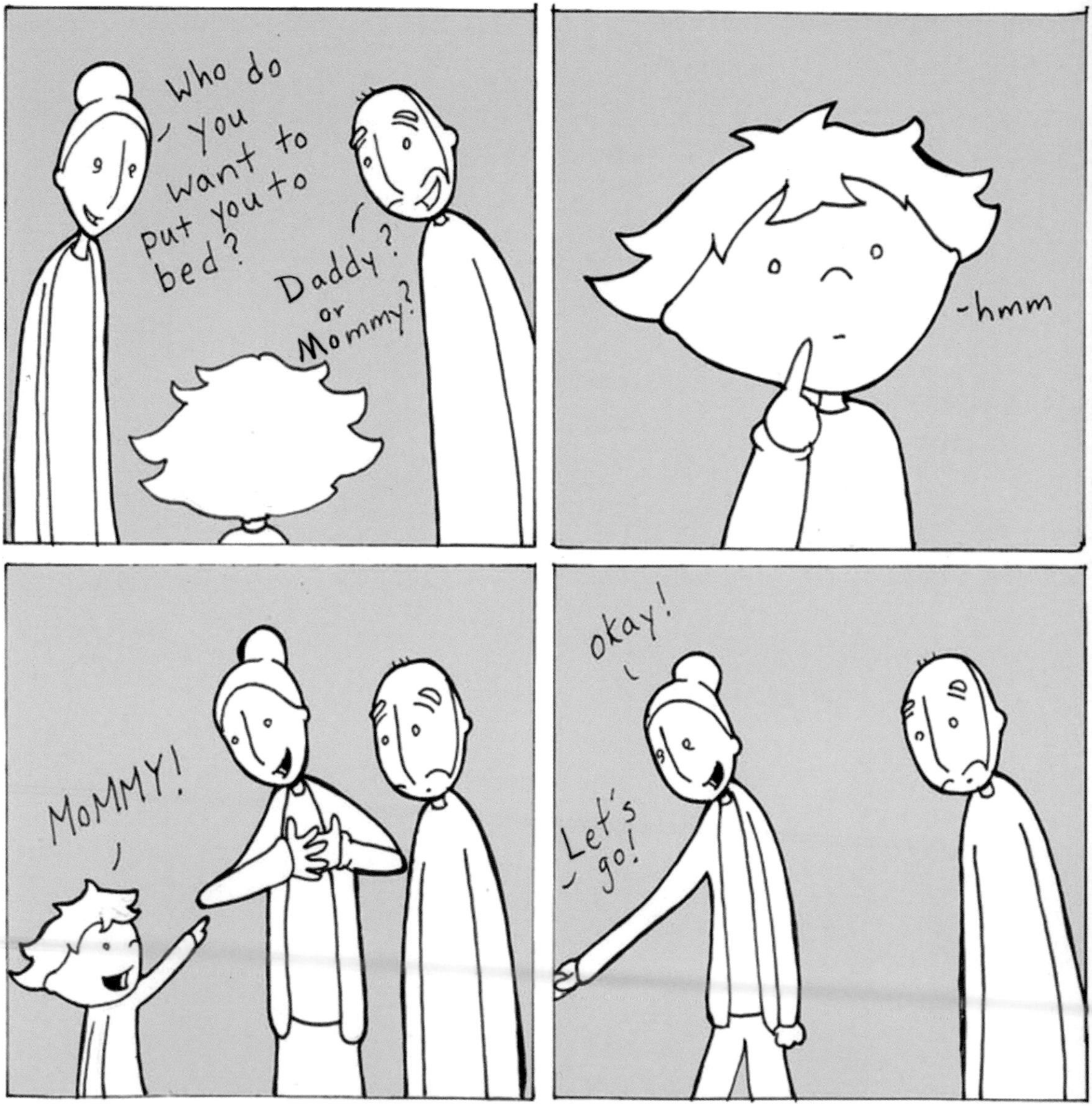
Who do you want to put you to bed?
Daddy? or Mommy?
-hmm
MOMMY!
okay!
Let's go!

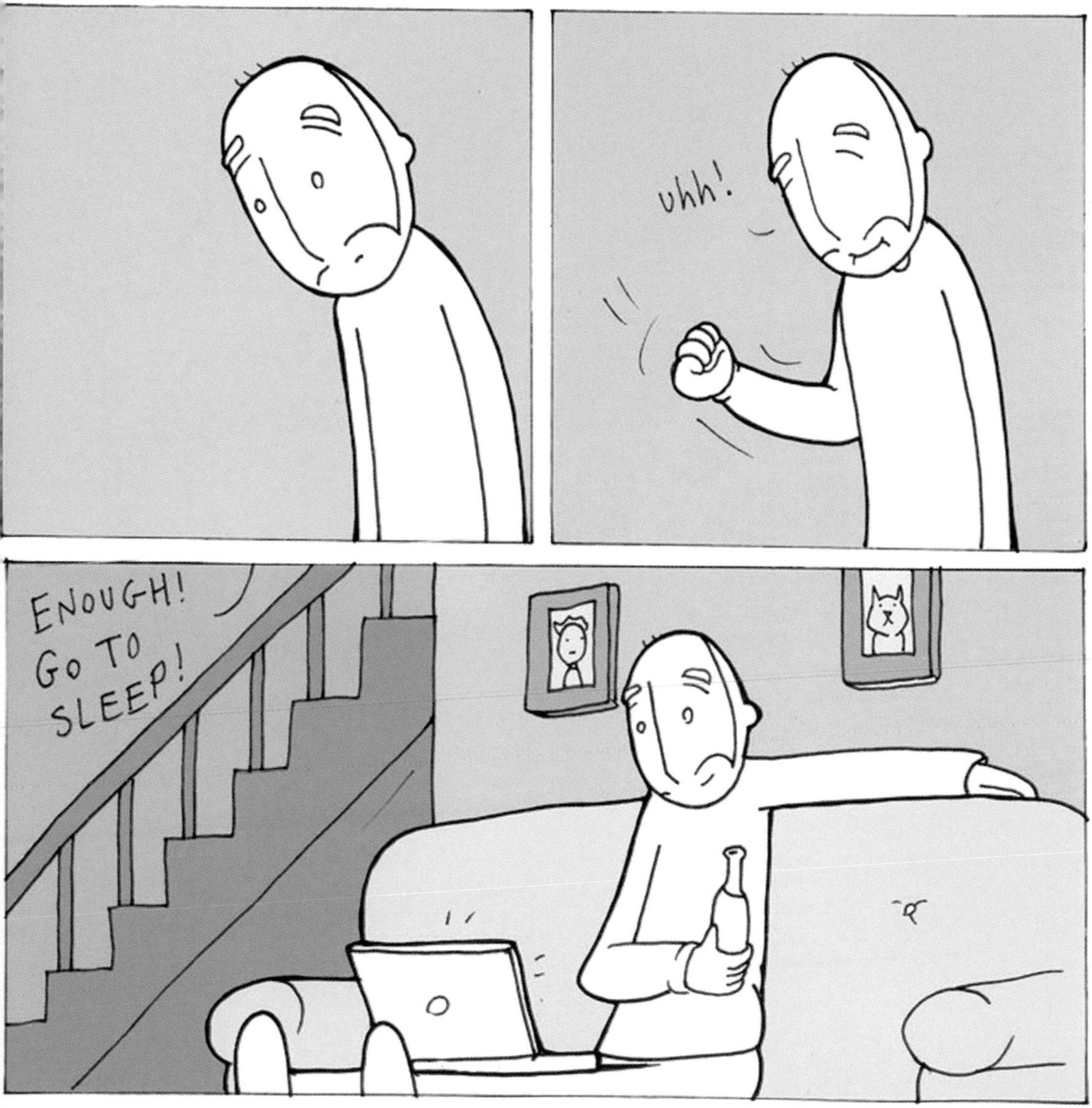
uhh!
ENOUGH! GO TO SLEEP!

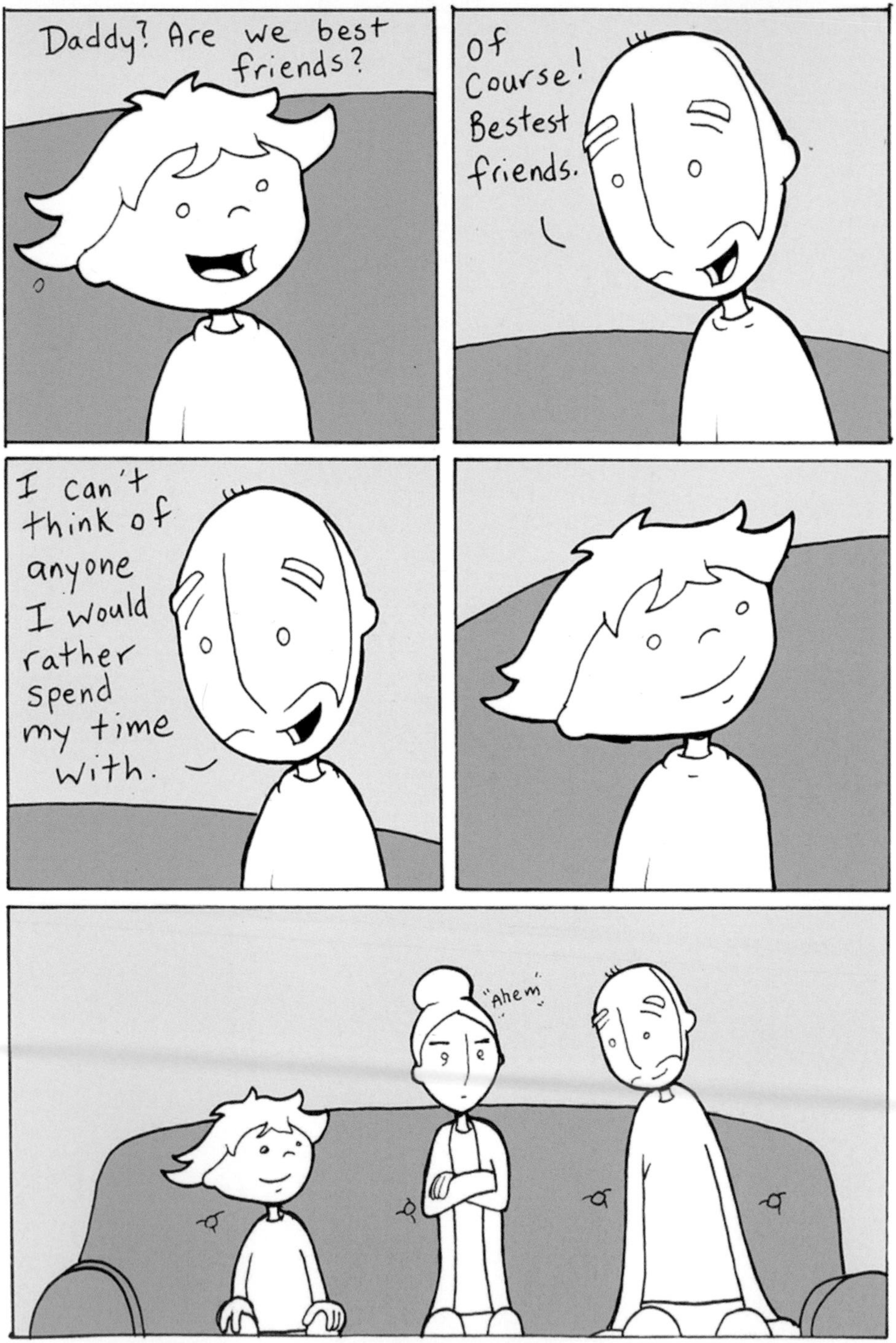
Daddy? Are we best friends?
Of Course! Bestest friends.
I can't think of anyone I would rather spend my time with.
"Ahem"

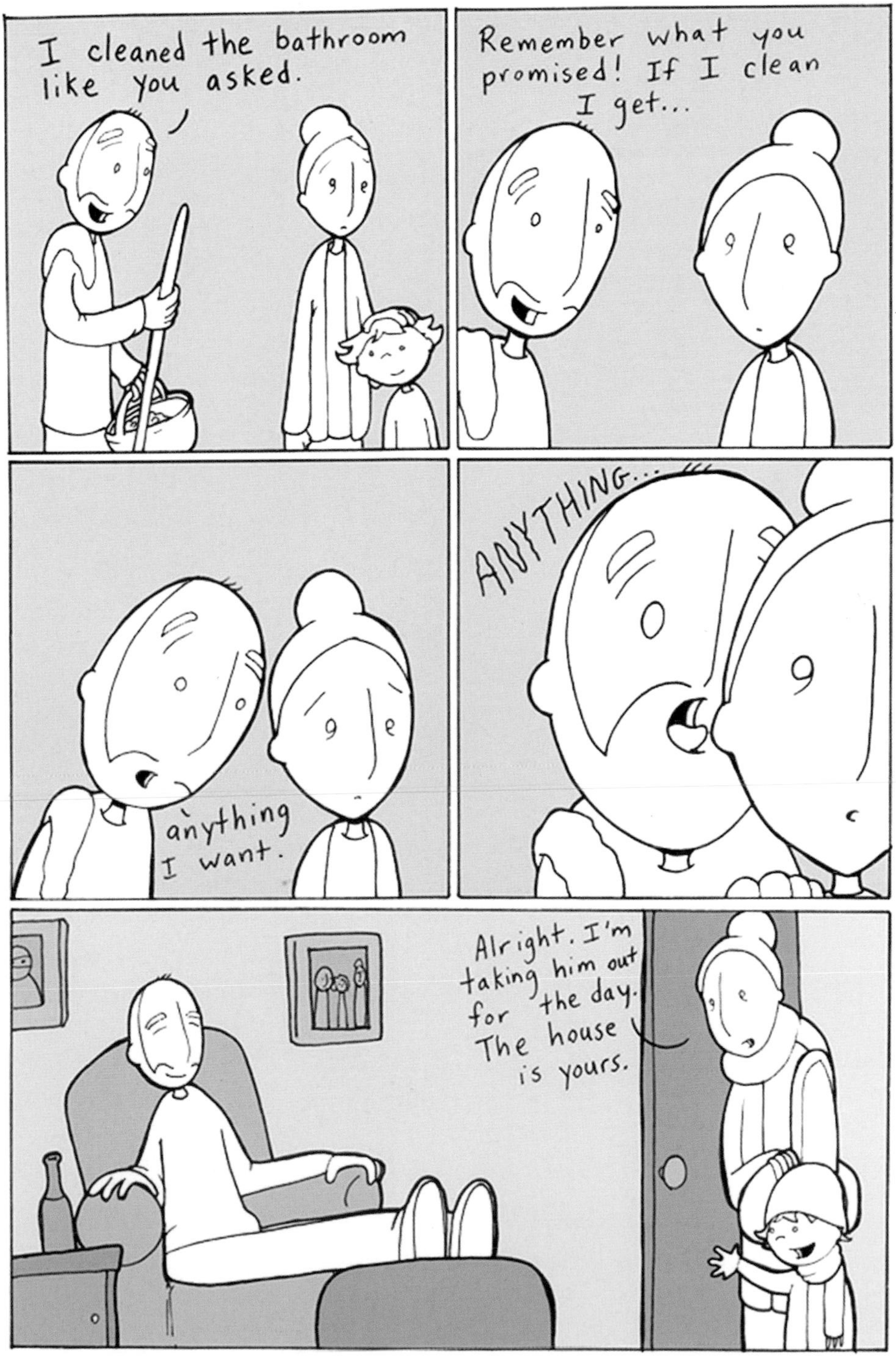
I cleaned the bathroom like you asked.
Remember what you promised! If I clean I get...
anything I want.
ANYTHING...
Alright. I'm taking him out for the day. The house is yours.

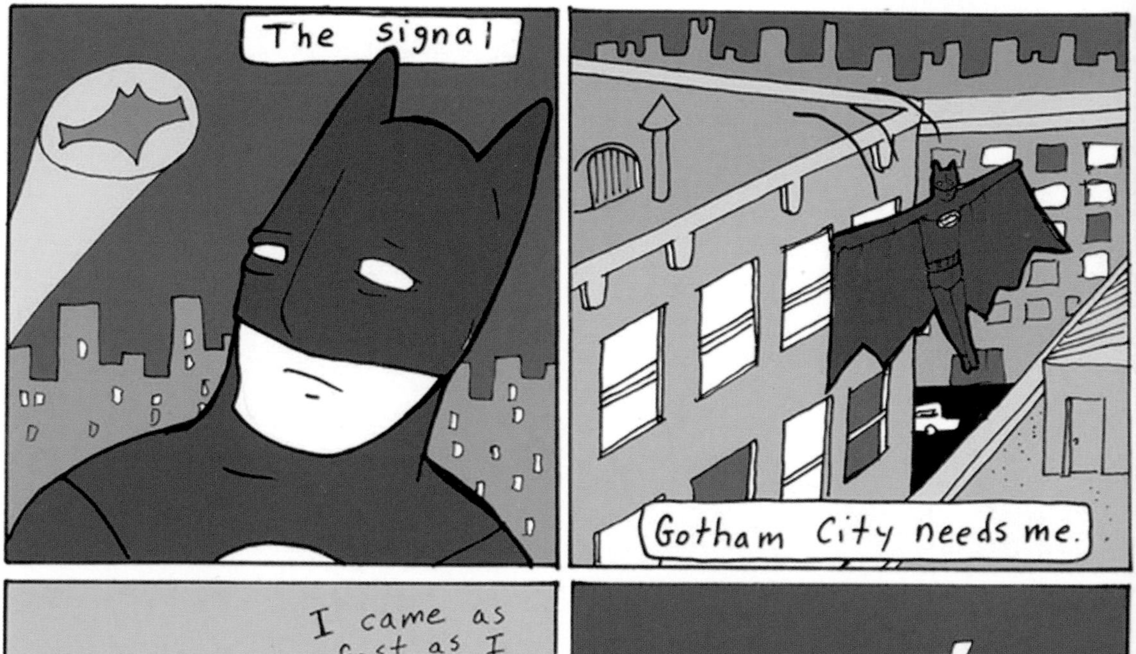
The signal
Gotham City needs me.
I came as fast as I could.
!

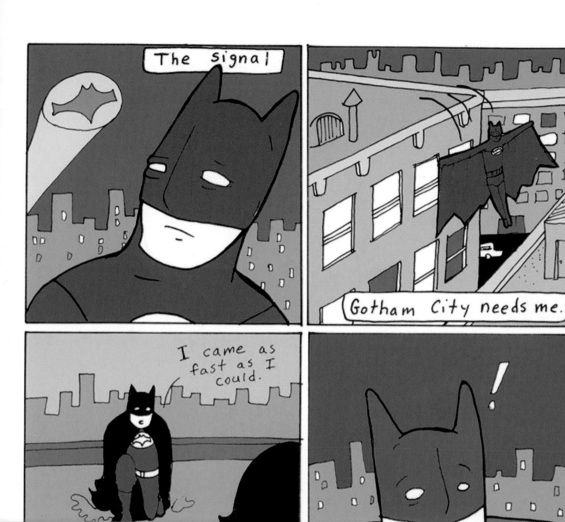

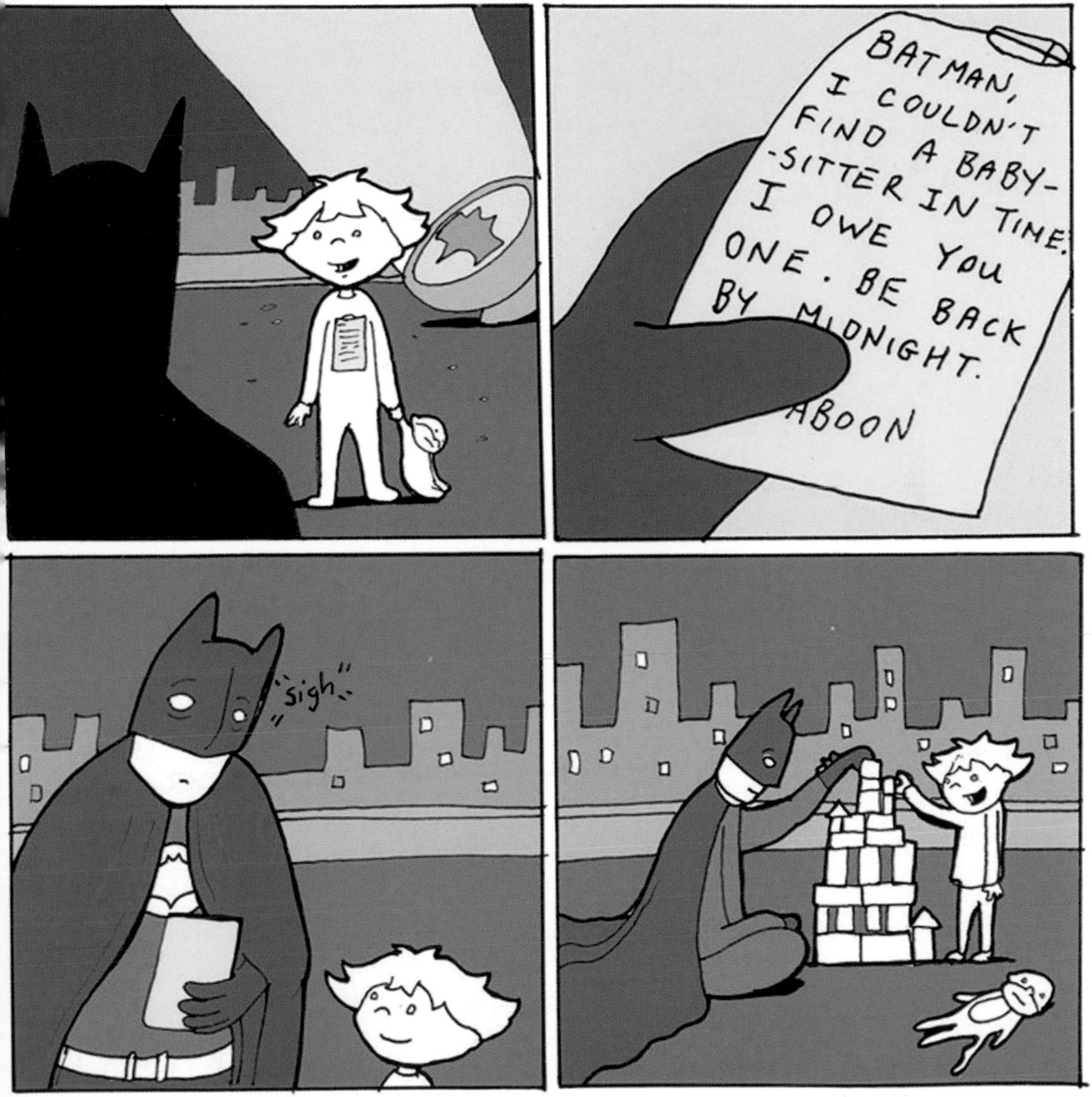
BATMAN,
I COULDN'T FIND A BABY-SITTER IN TIME.
I OWE YOU ONE. BE BACK BY MIDNIGHT.
ABOON
sigh

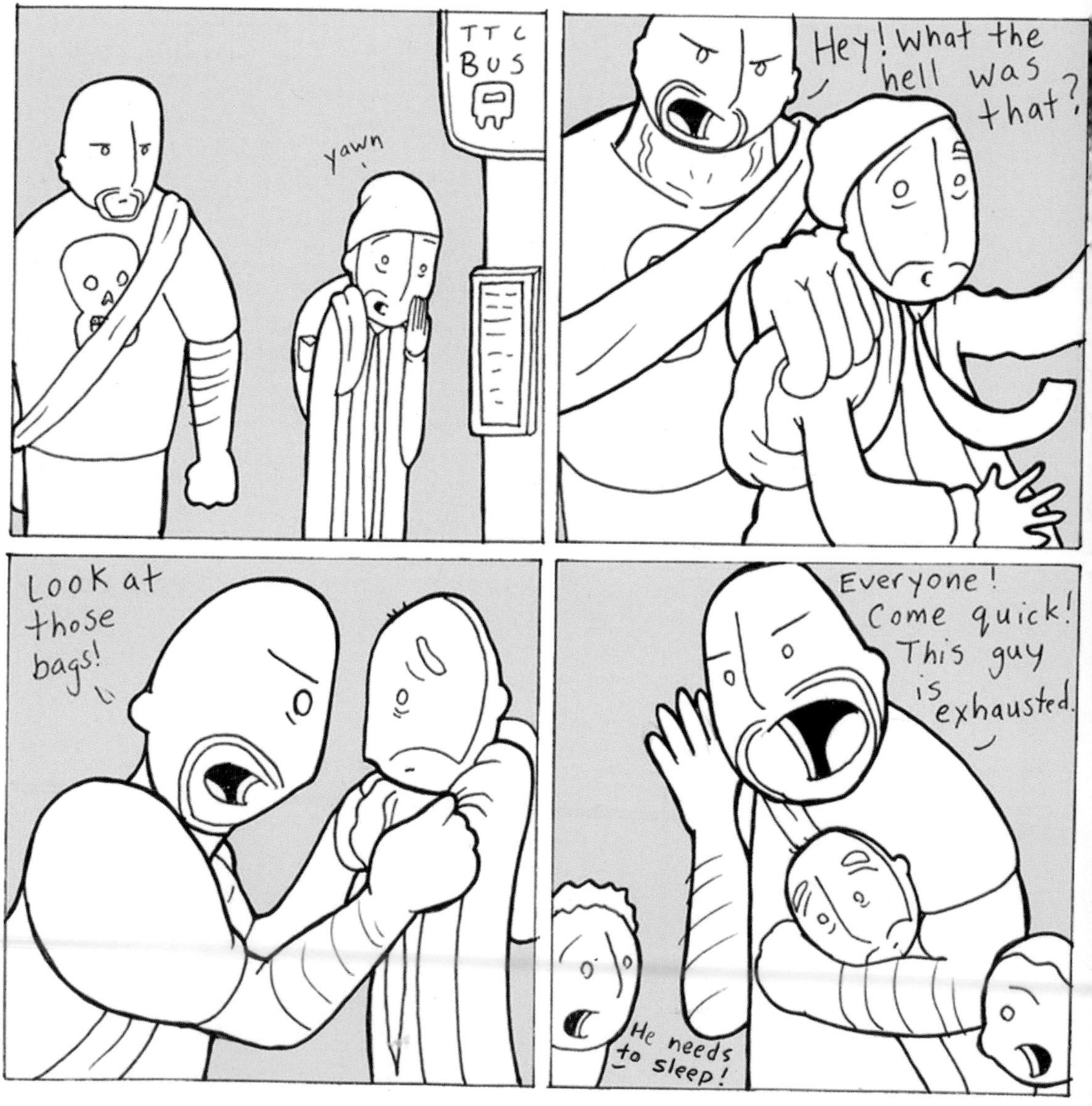
TTC
BUS
yawn
Hey! What the hell was that?
Look at those bags!
Everyone! Come quick! This guy is exhausted.
He needs to sleep!

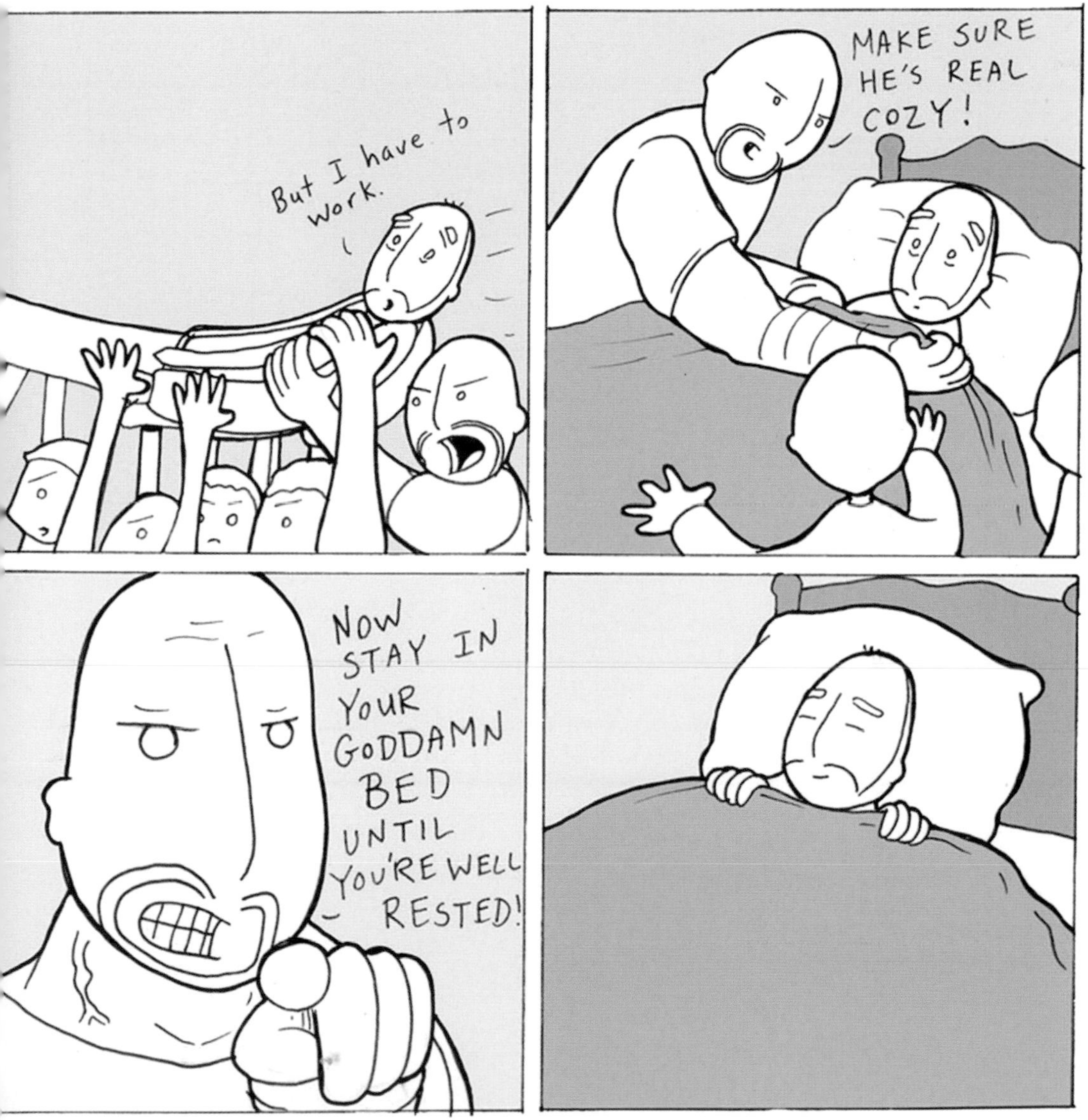
But I have to work.
MAKE SURE HE'S REAL COZY!
NOW STAY IN YOUR GODDAMN BED UNTIL YOU'RE WELL RESTED!

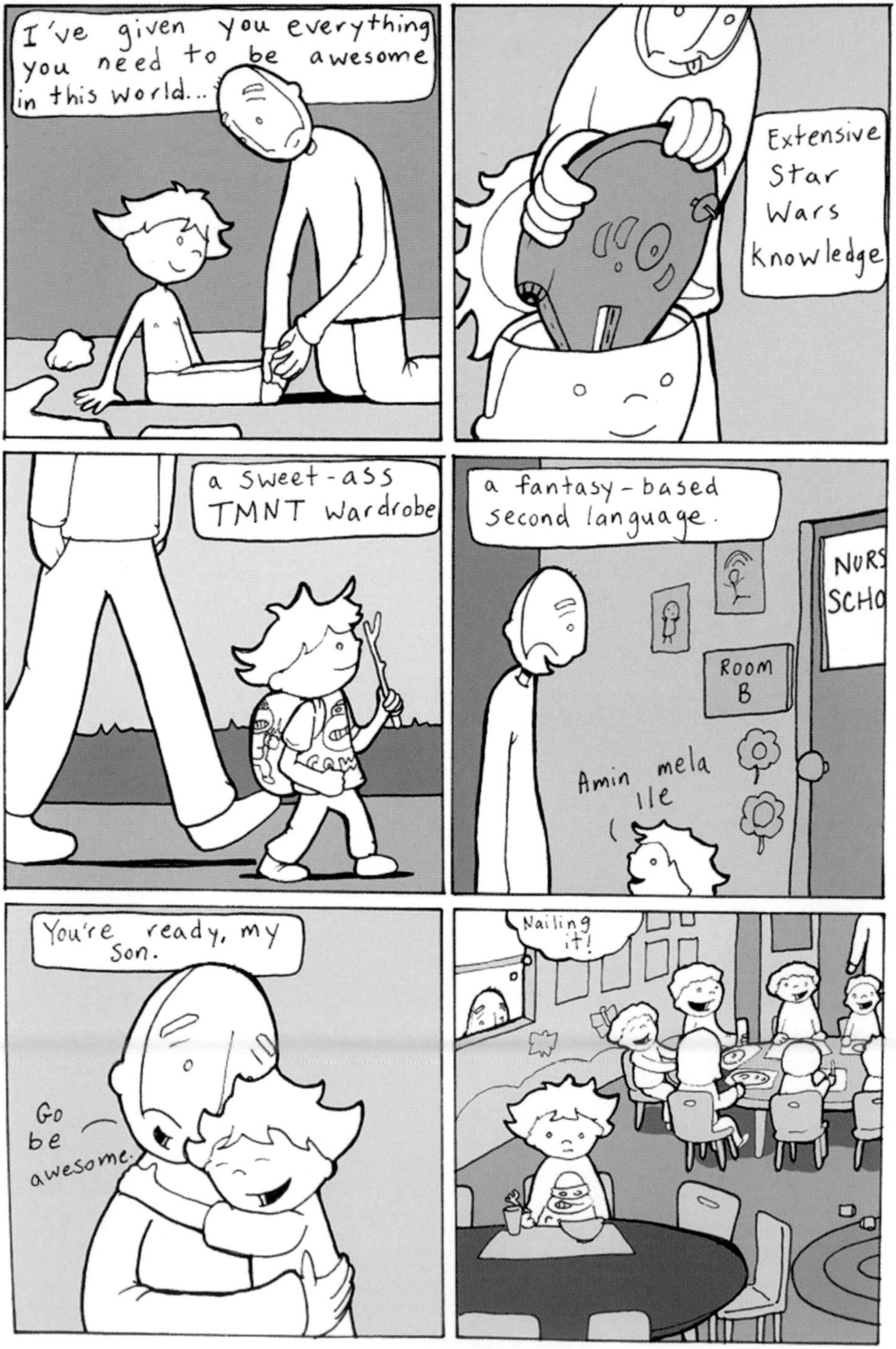
I've given you everything you need to be awesome in this world...
Extensive Star Wars knowledge
a sweet-ass TMNT wardrobe
a fantasy-based second language.
NURS
SCHO
ROOM B
Amin mela lle
You're ready, my son.
Go be awesome.
Nailing it!

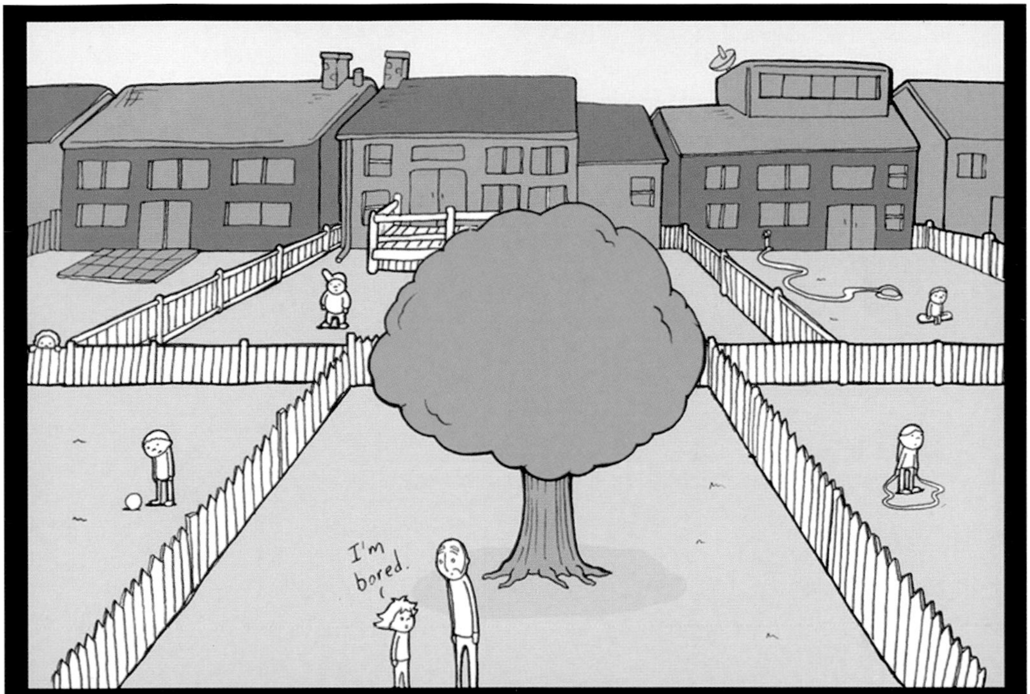
I'm bored.

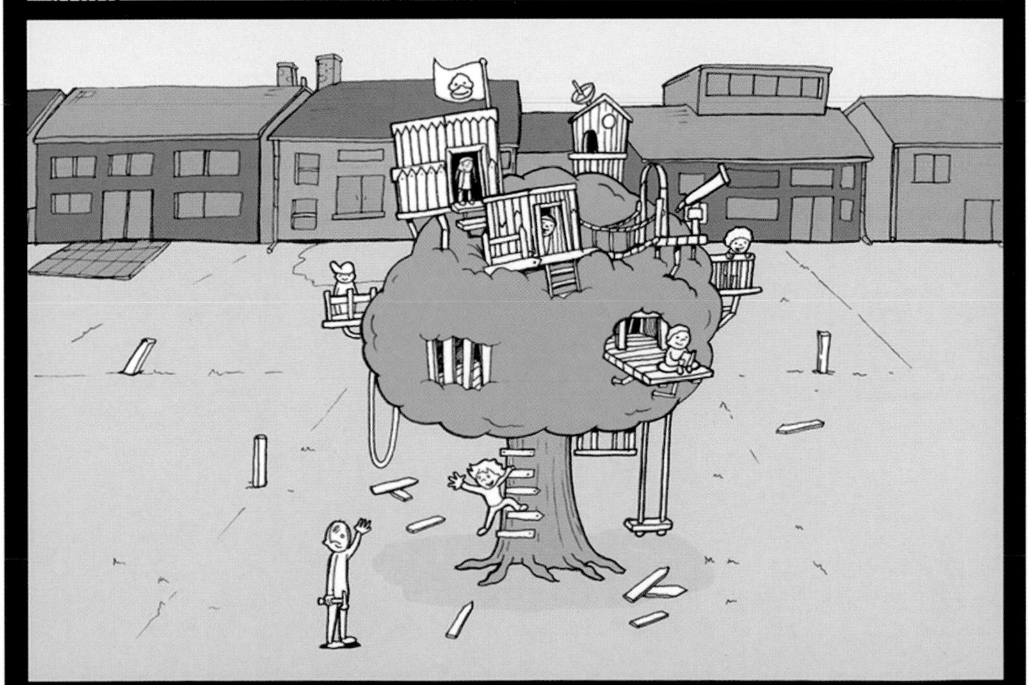

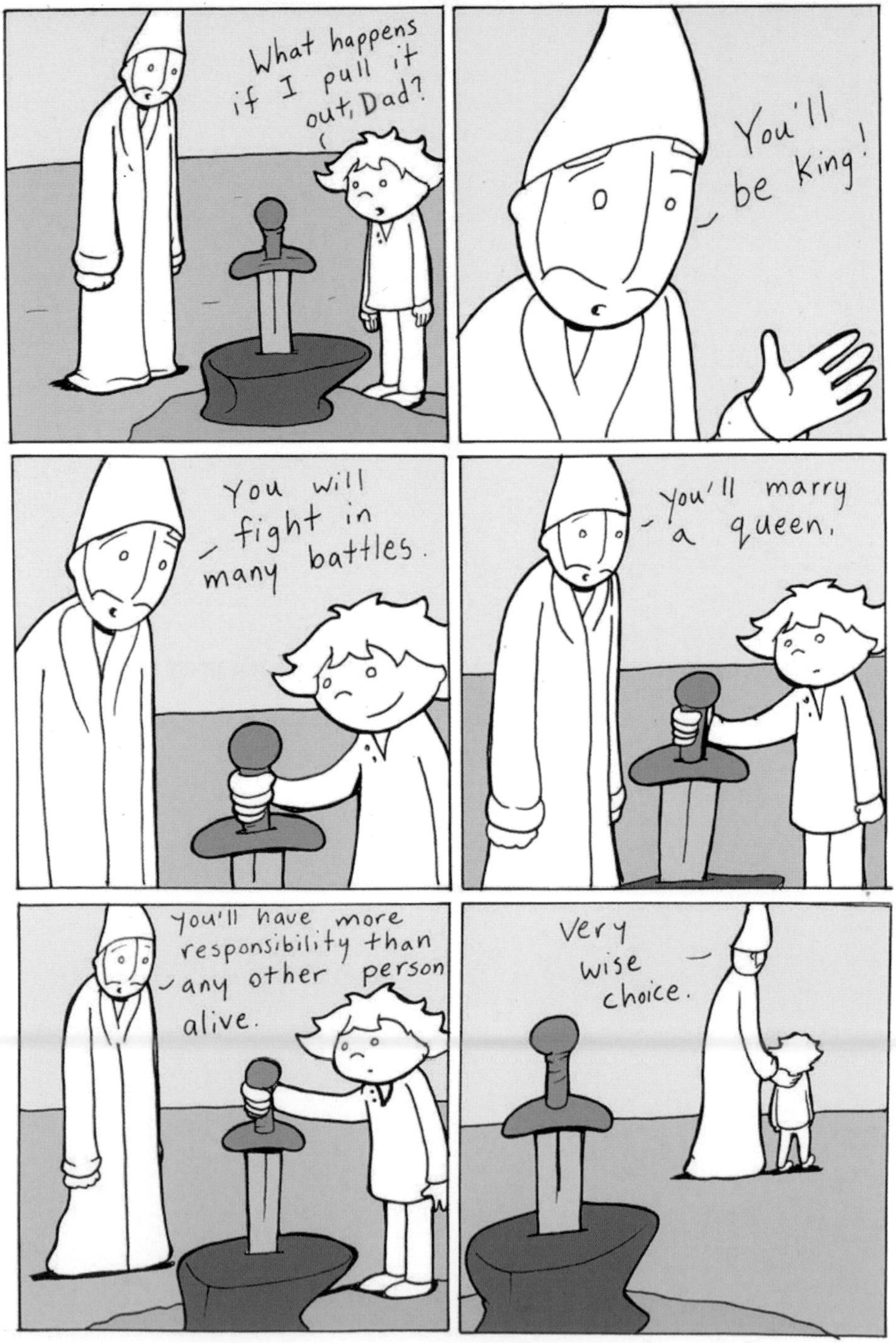
What happens if I pull it out, Dad?
You'll be King!
You will fight in many battles.
You'll marry a queen.
You'll have more responsibility than any other person alive.
Very wise choice.

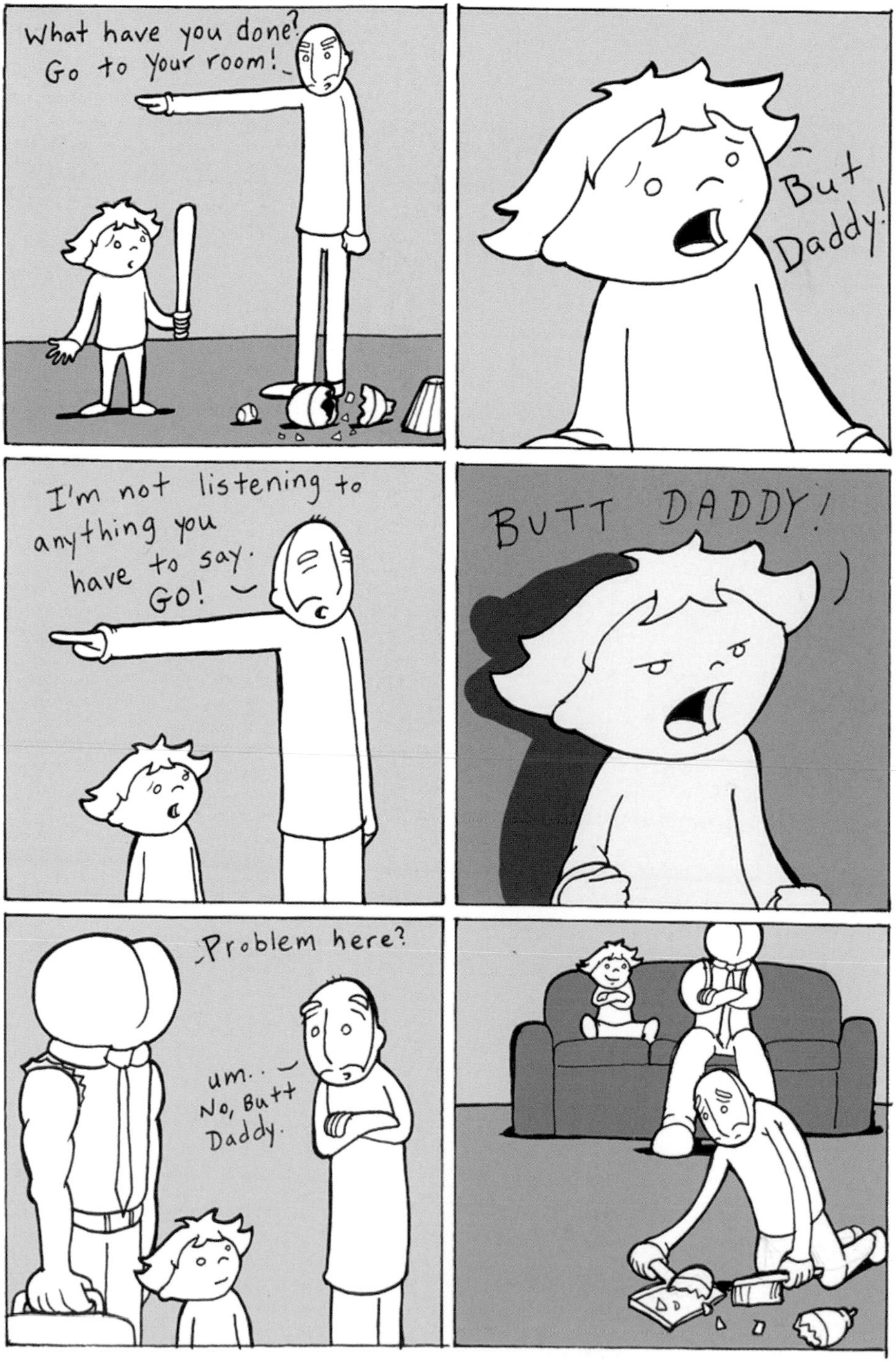
What have you done? Go to your room!
But Daddy!
I'm not listening to anything you have to say. GO!
BUTT DADDY!
Problem here?
um.. No, Butt Daddy.

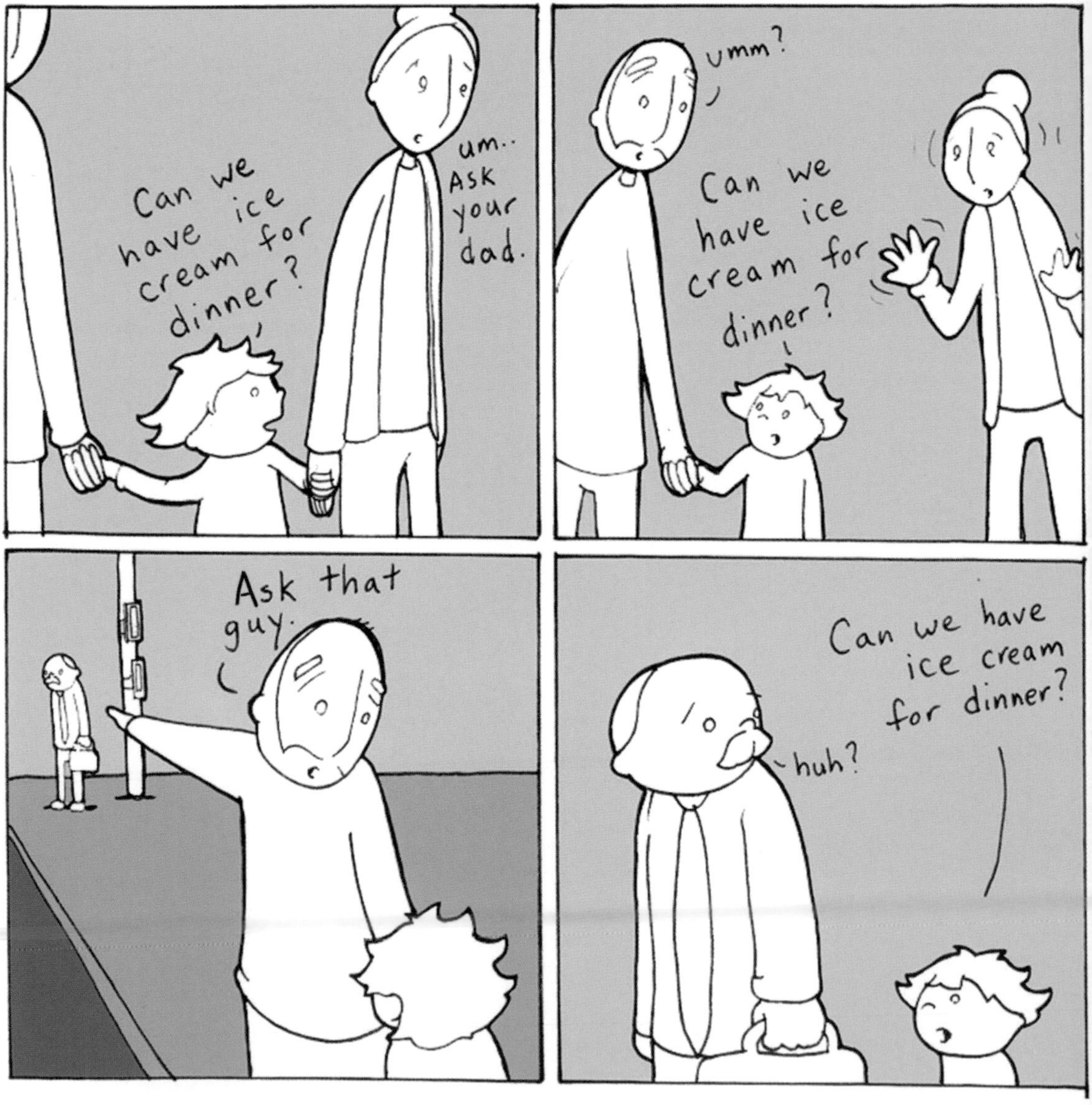
Can we have ice cream for dinner?
um.. Ask your dad.
umm?
Can we have ice cream for dinner?
Ask that guy.
huh?
Can we have ice cream for dinner?

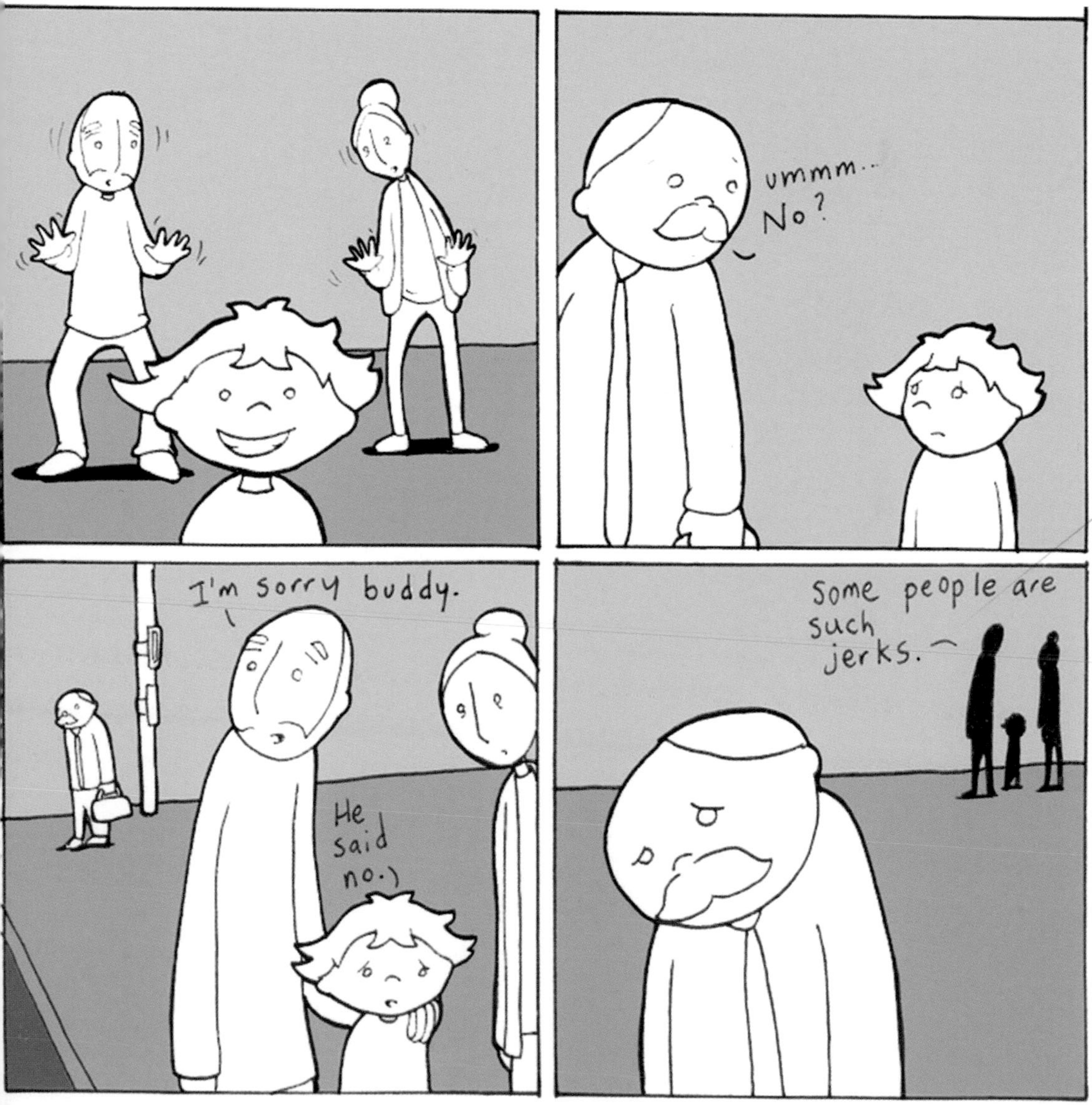
ummm...
No?
I'm sorry buddy.
He said no.
Some people are such jerks.

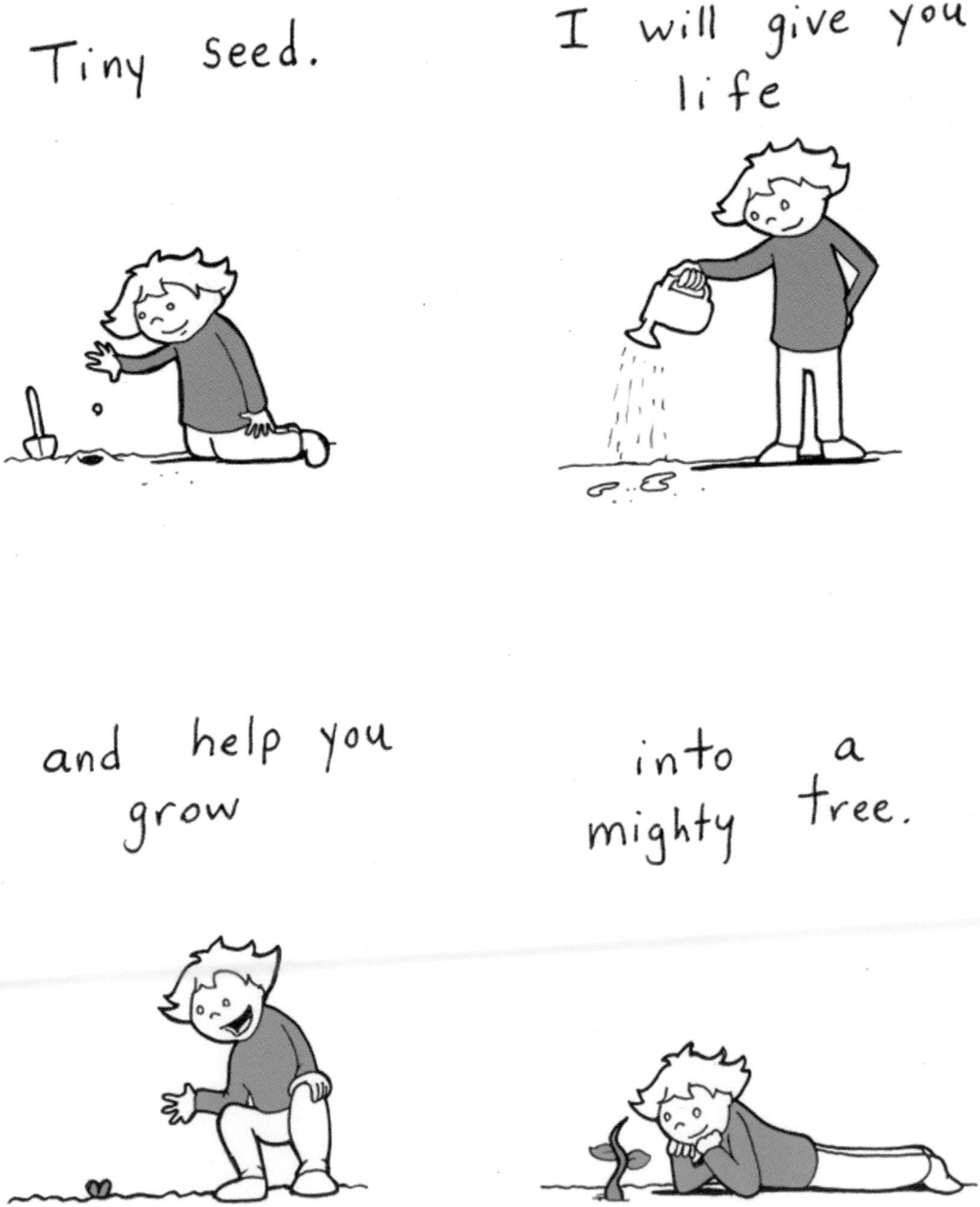
Tiny seed.
I will give you life
and help you grow
into a mighty tree.

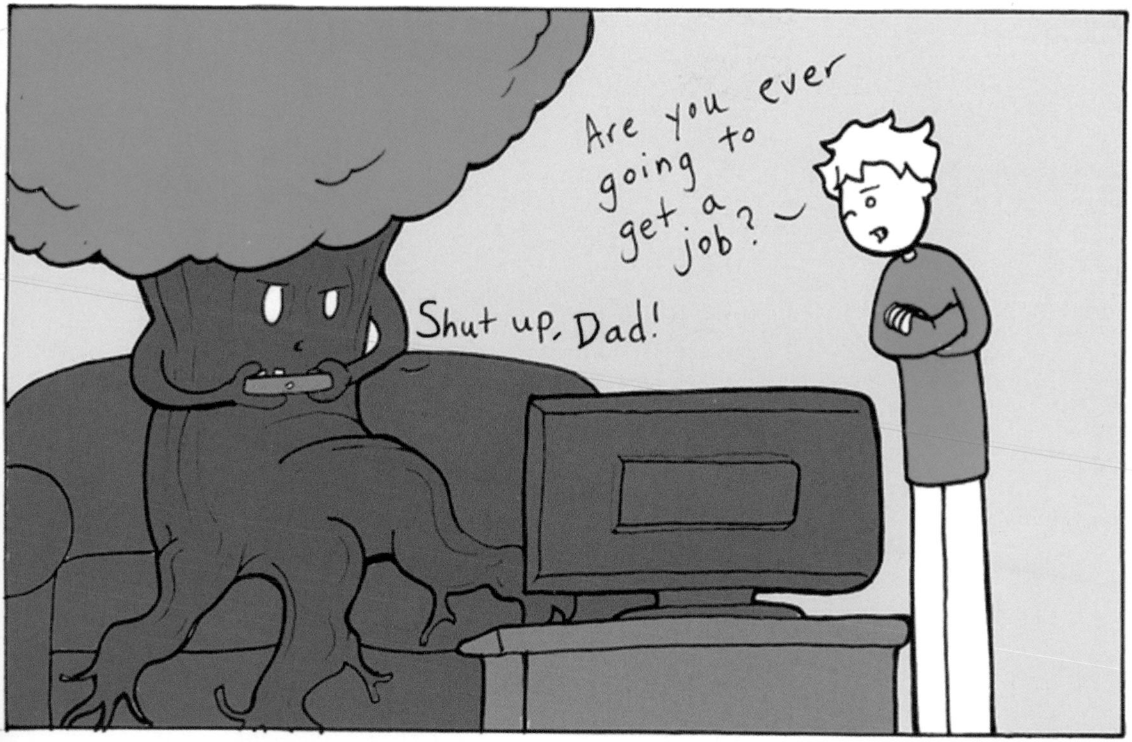
Are you ever going to get a job?
Shut up, Dad!

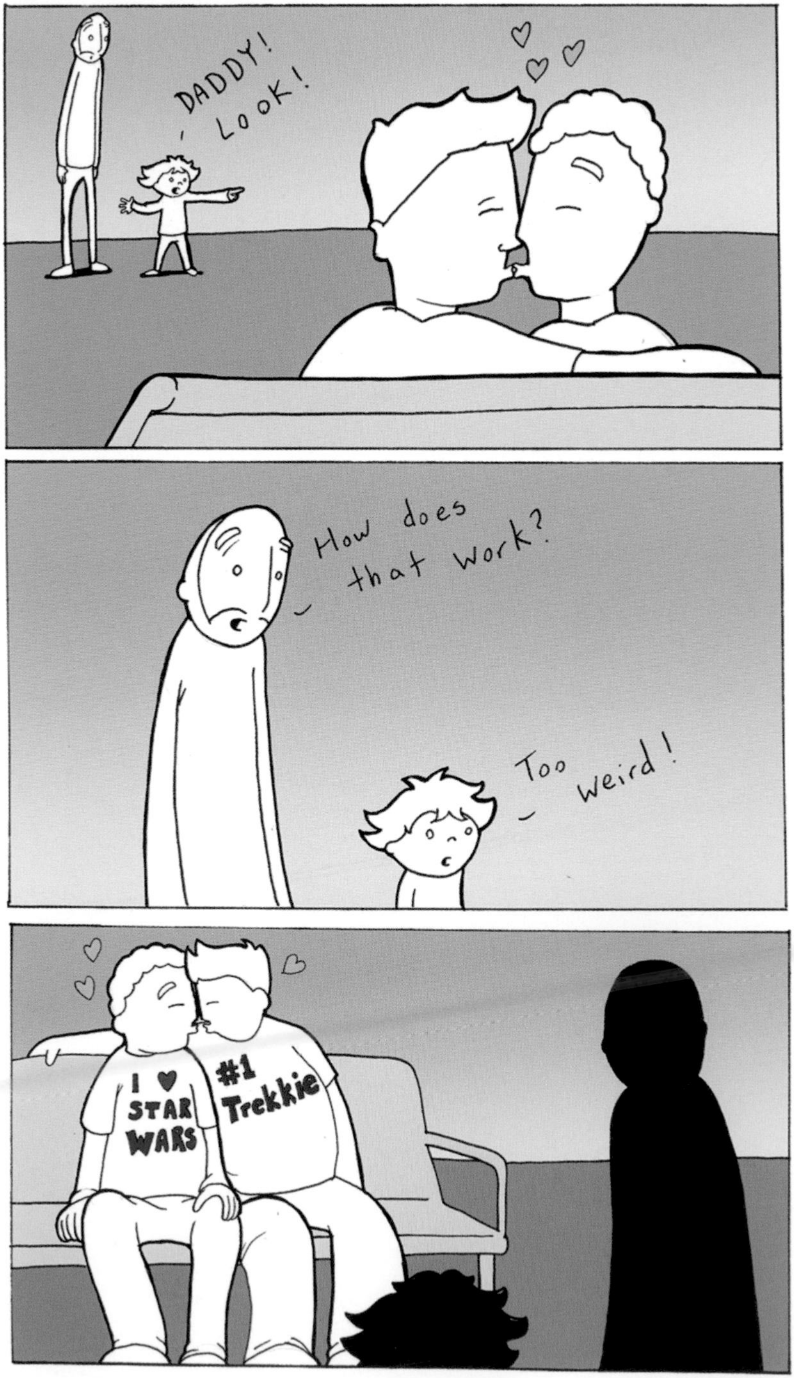
DADDY! LOOK!
How does that work?
Too weird!
I ♥ STAR WARS
#1 Trekkie

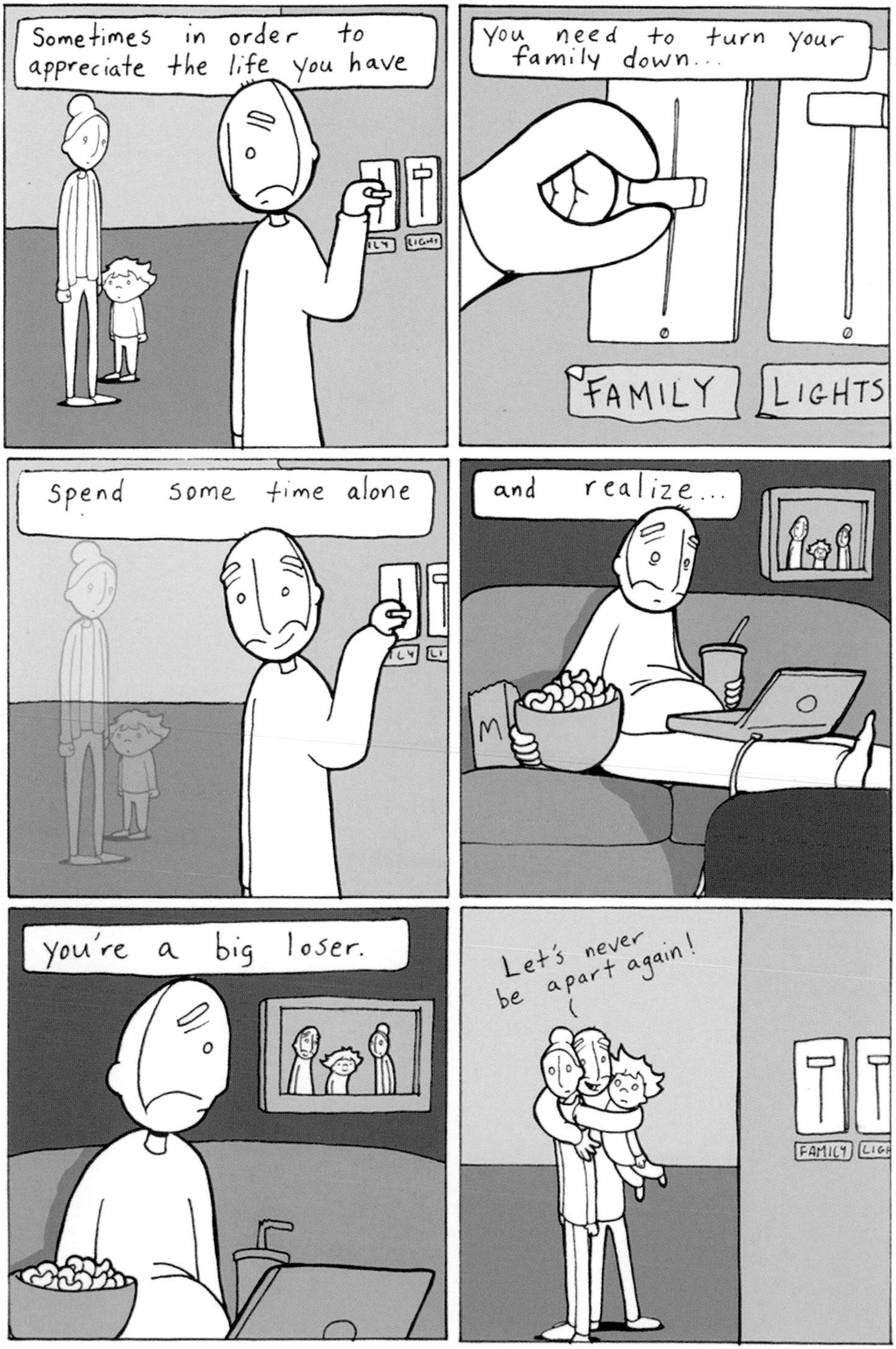
Sometimes in order to appreciate the life you have
You need to turn your family down...
FAMILY
LIGHTS
spend some time alone
and realize...
you're a big loser.
Let's never be apart again!
FAMILY

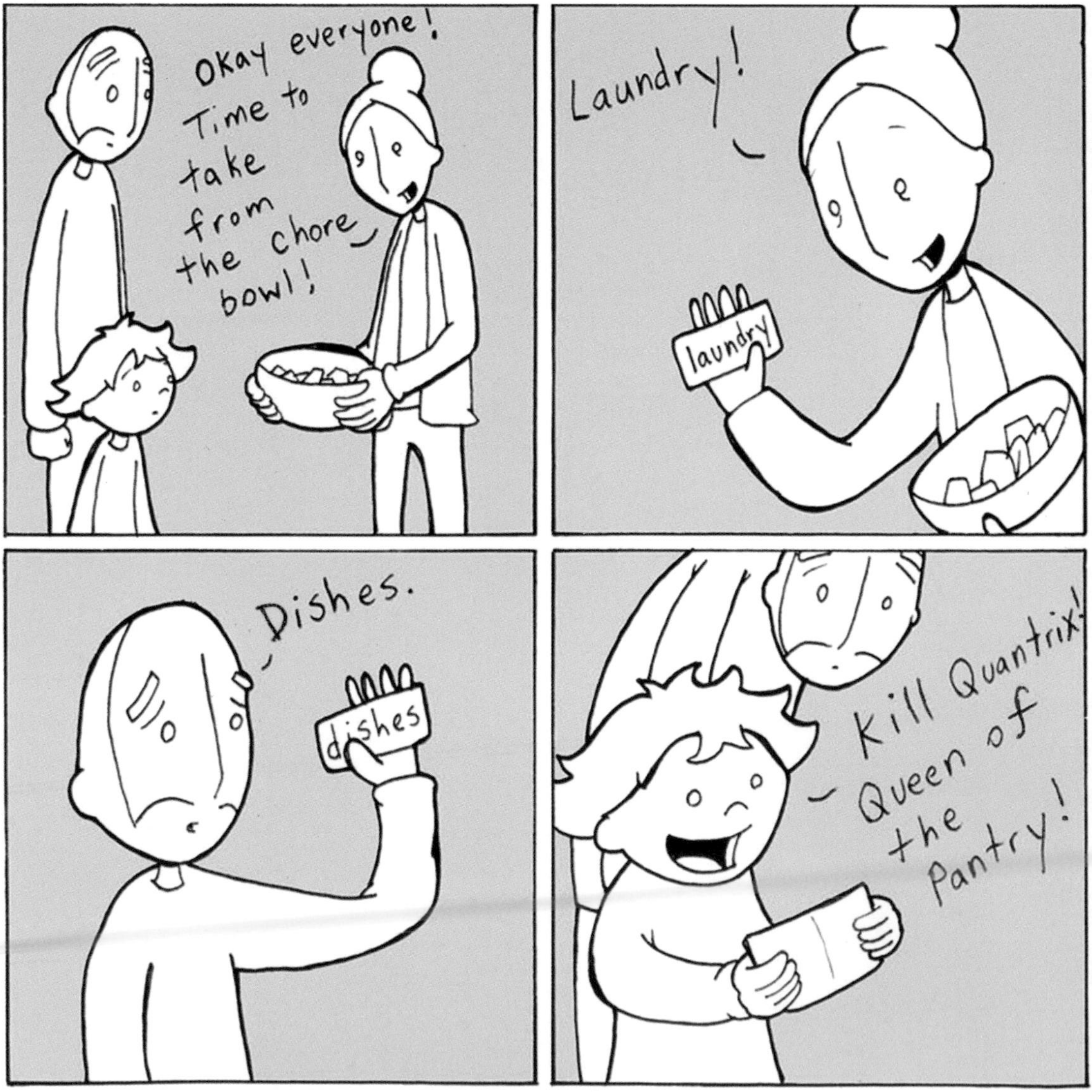
Okay everyone! Time to take from the chore bowl!
laundry
Laundry!
dishes
Dishes.
Kill Quantrix! Queen of the Pantry!

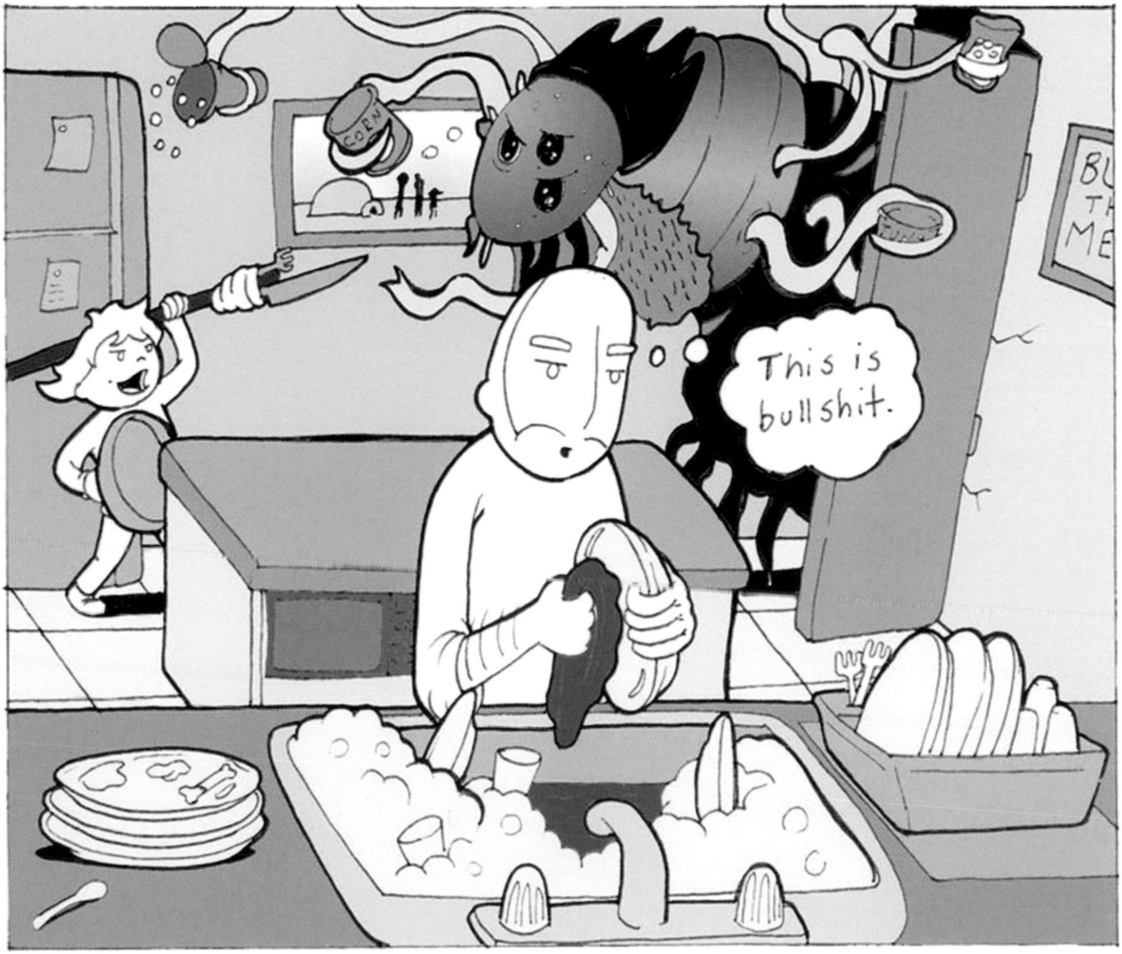
CORN
This is bullshit.

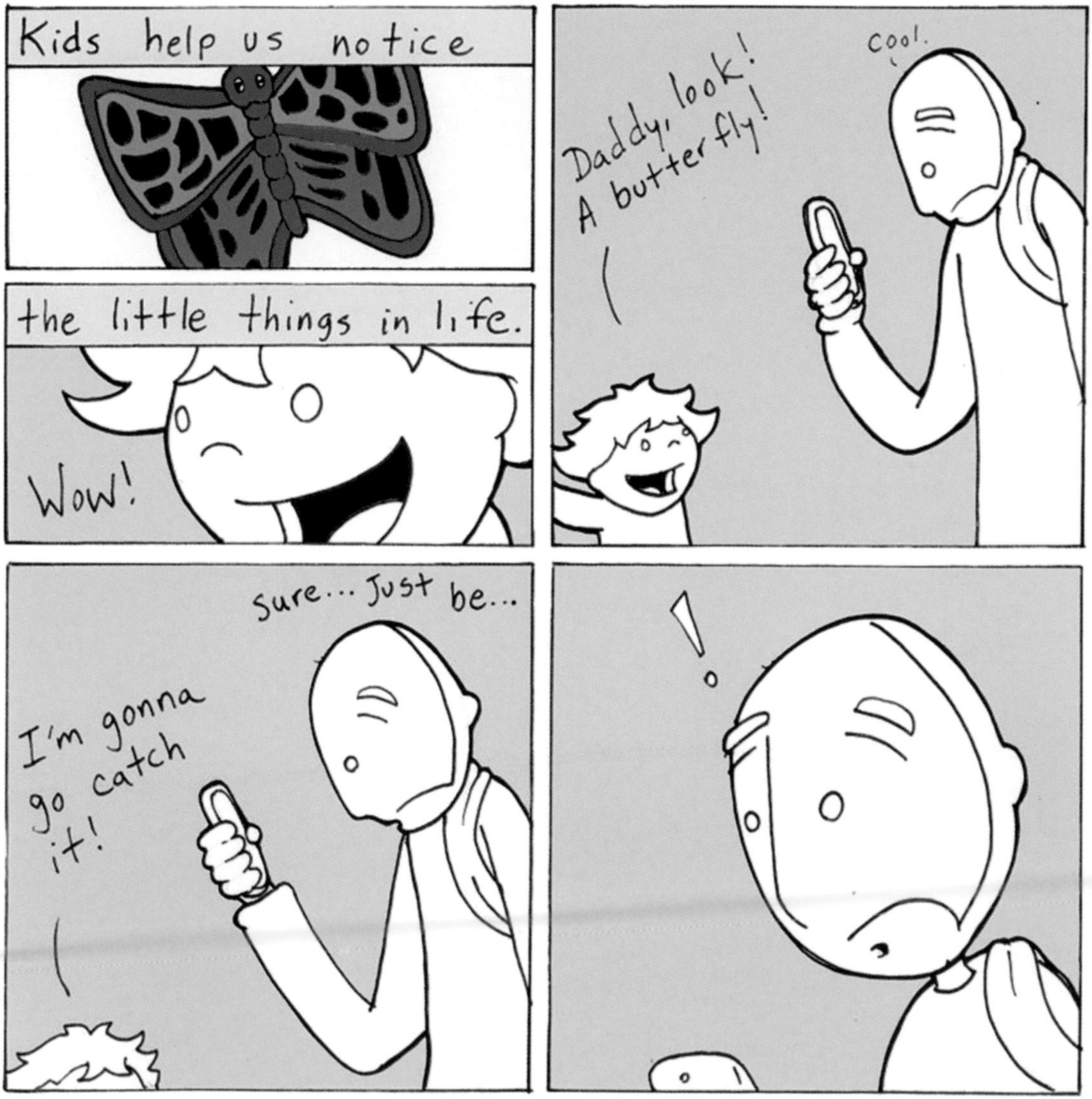
Kids help us notice
the little things in life.
Wow!
Daddy, look! A butterfly!
Cool.
I'm gonna go catch it!
Sure... Just be...
!

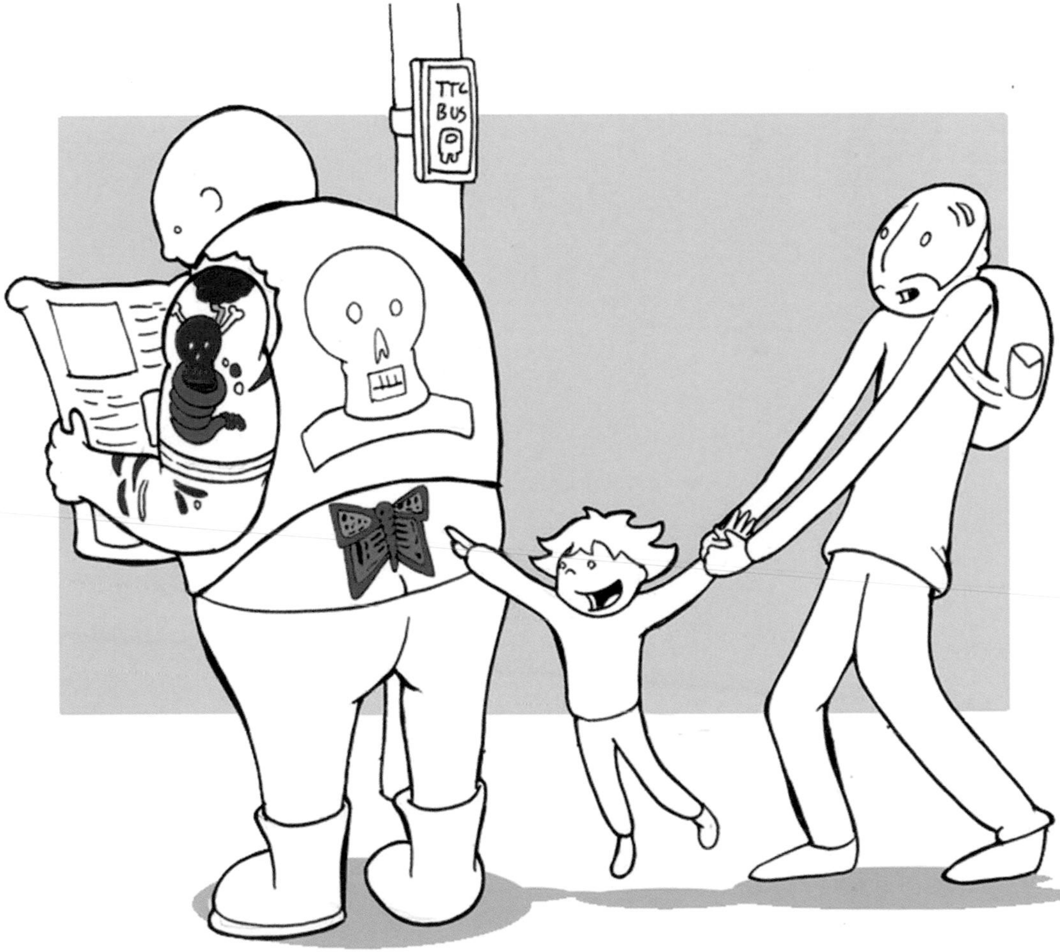
TTC
BUS

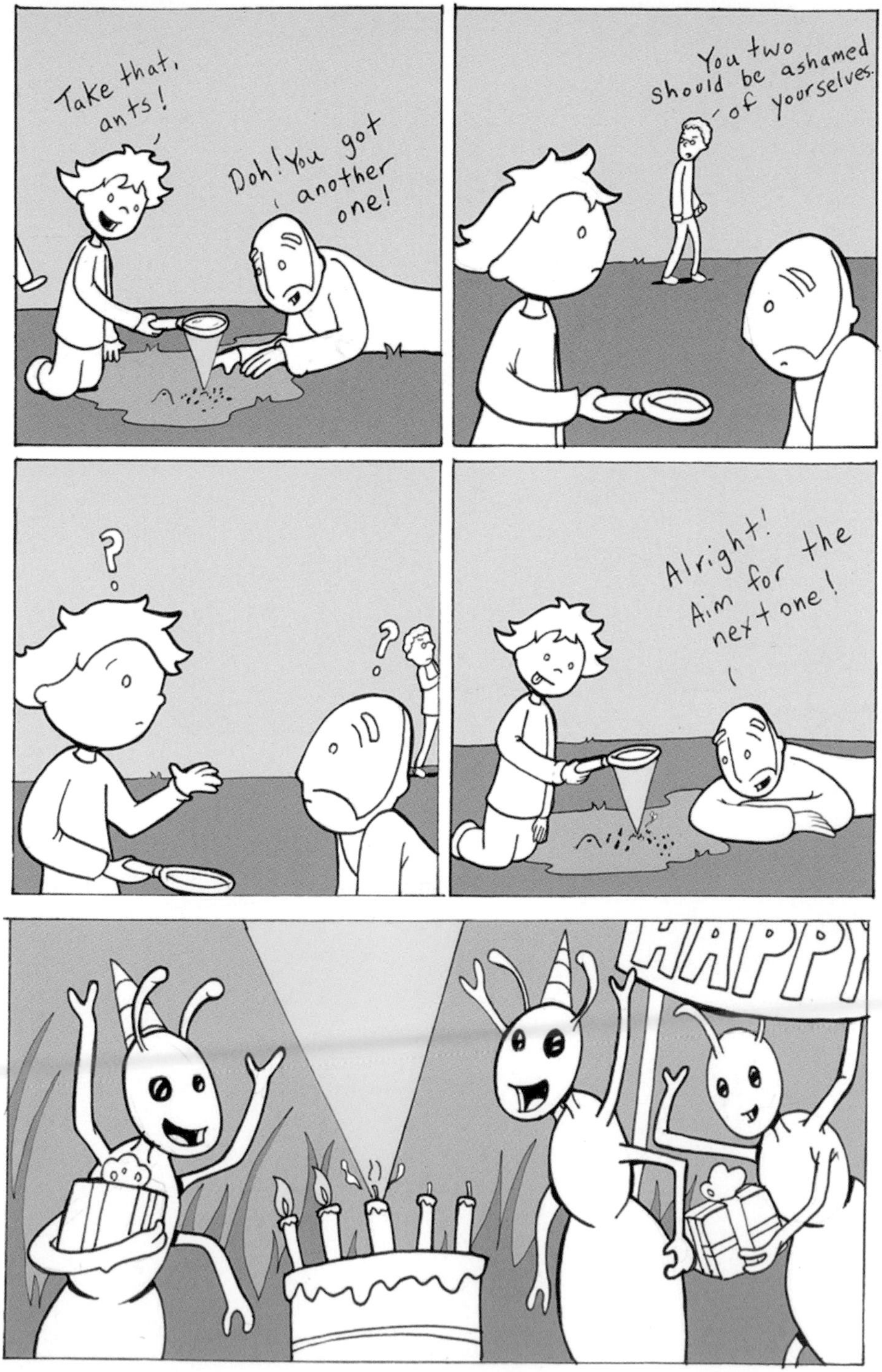
Take that, ants!
Doh! You got another one!
You two should be ashamed of yourselves.
?
?
Alright! Aim for the next one!
HAPPY

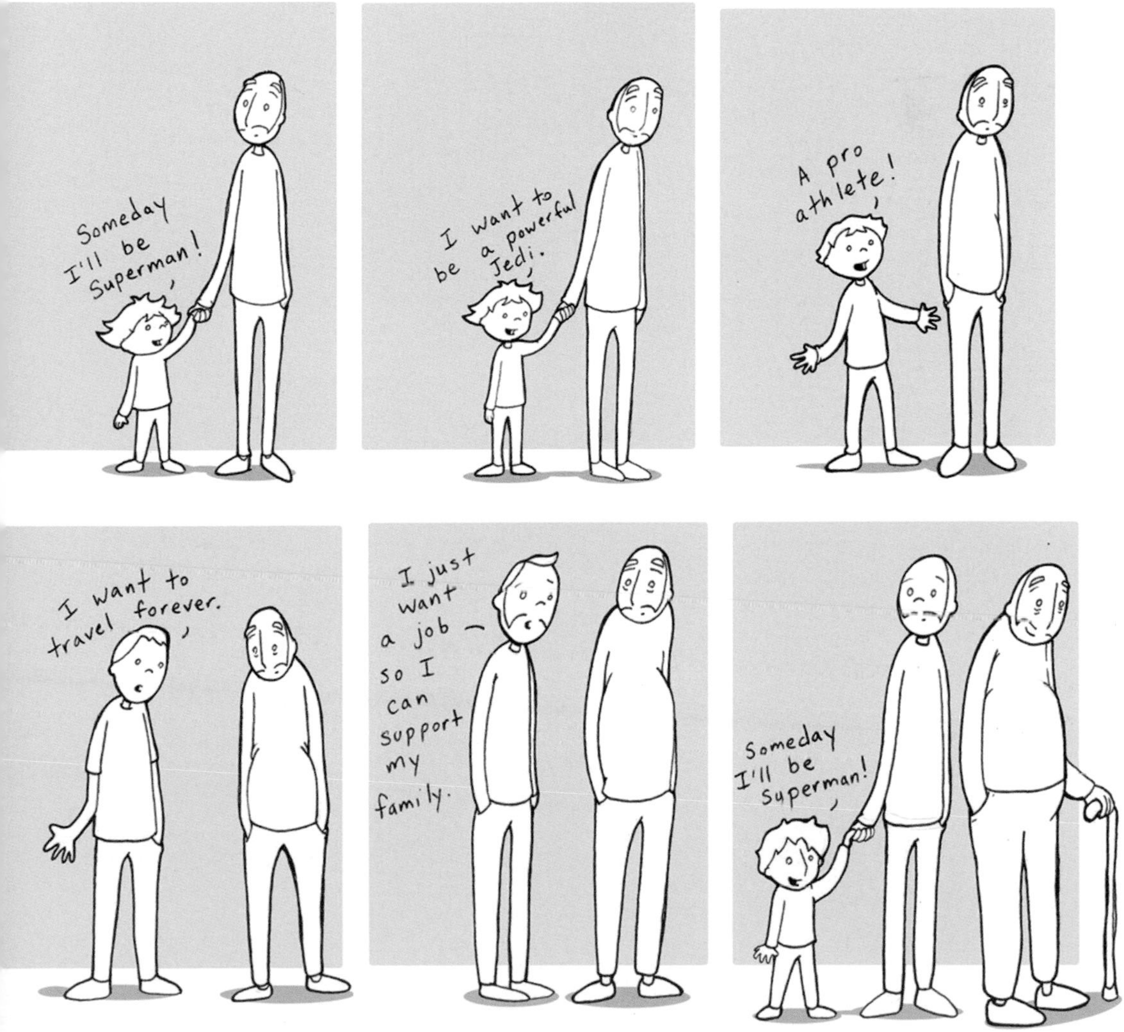
Someday I'll be Superman!
I want to be a powerful Jedi.
A pro athlete!
I want to travel forever.
I just want a job — so I can support my family.
Someday I'll be Superman!

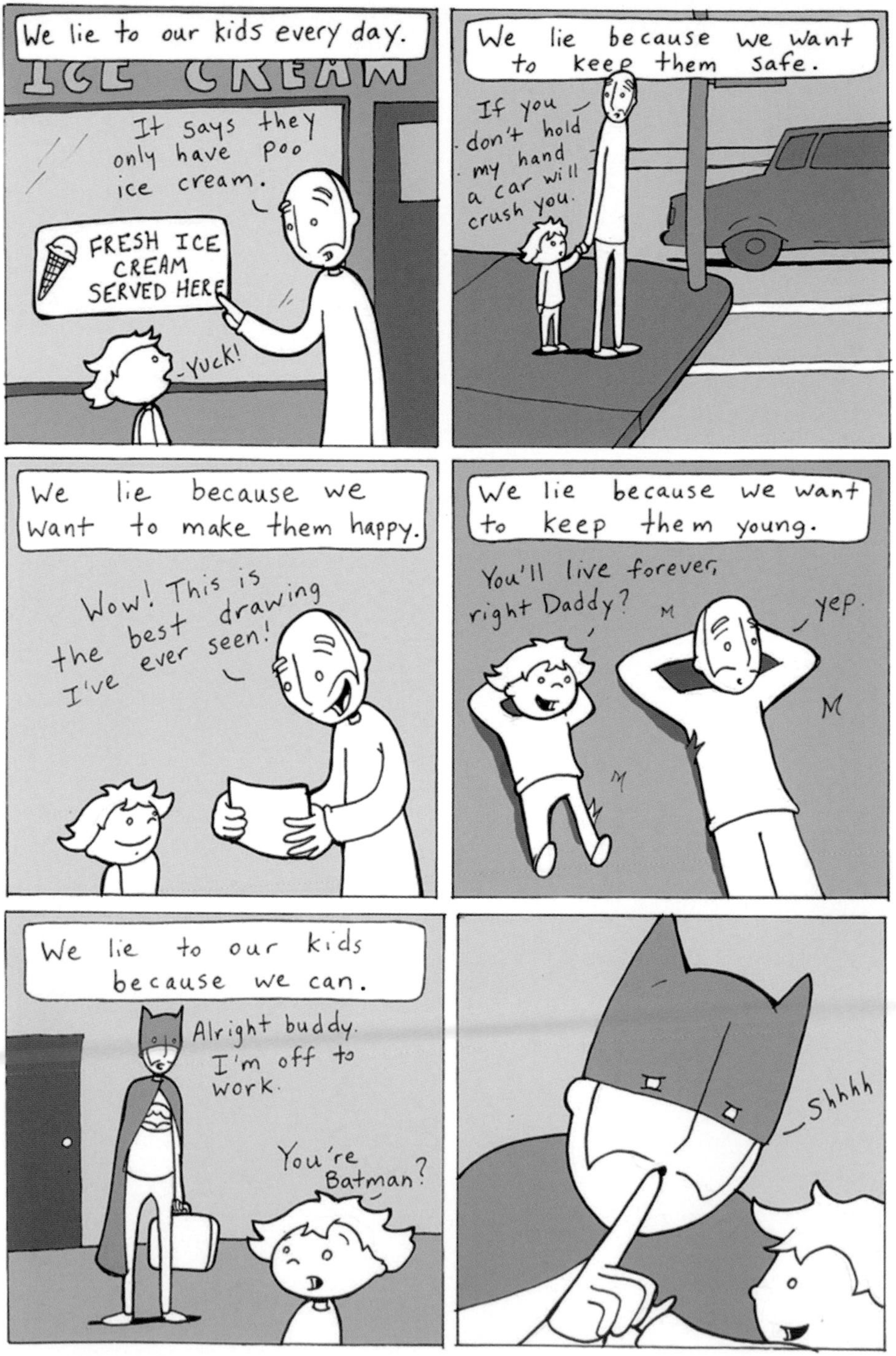
We lie to our kids every day.
ICE CREAM
It says they only have poo ice cream.
FRESH ICE CREAM SERVED HERE
Yuck!
We lie because we want to keep them safe.
If you don't hold my hand a car will crush you.
We lie because we want to make them happy.
Wow! This is the best drawing I've ever seen!
We lie because we want to keep them young.
You'll live forever, right Daddy?
Yep.
We lie to our kids because we can.
Alright buddy. I'm off to work.
You're Batman?
Shhhh

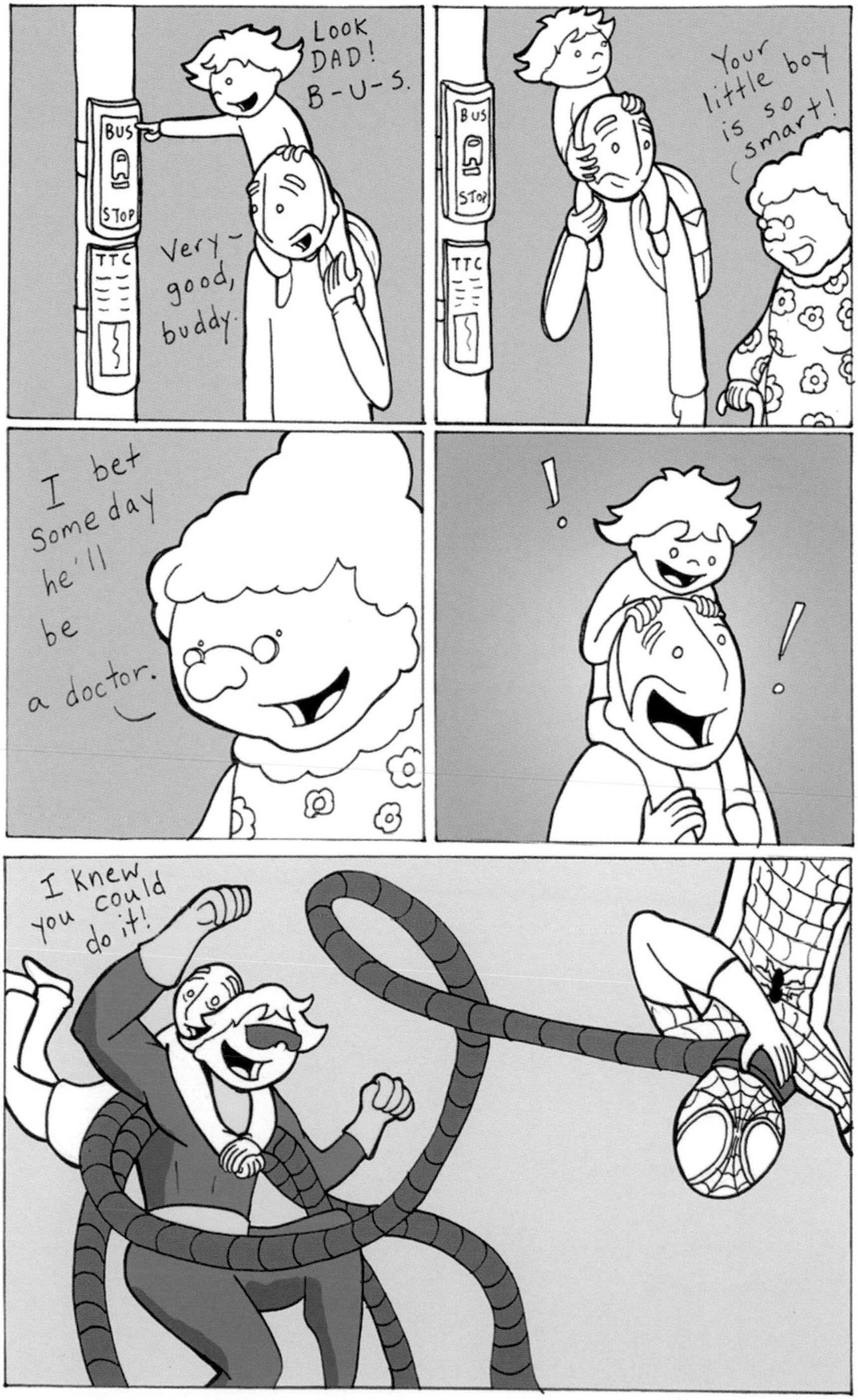
LOOK DAD! B-U-S.
BUS STOP
TTC
Very good, buddy.
BUS STOP
TTC
Your little boy is so smart!
I bet someday he'll be a doctor.
!
!
I knew you could do it!

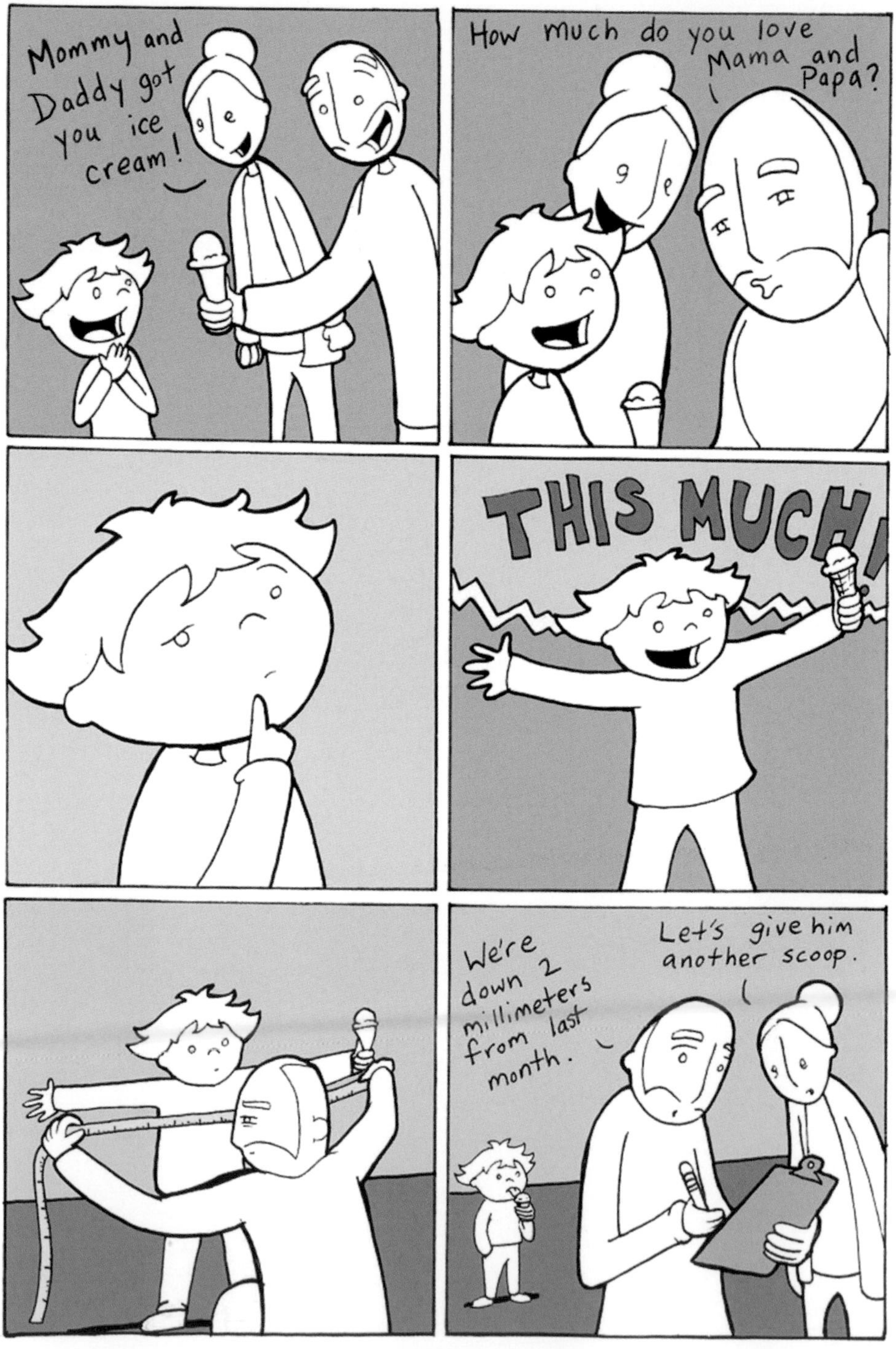
Mommy and Daddy got you ice cream!
How much do you love Mama and Papa?
THIS MUCH!
We're down 2 millimeters from last month.
Let's give him another scoop.

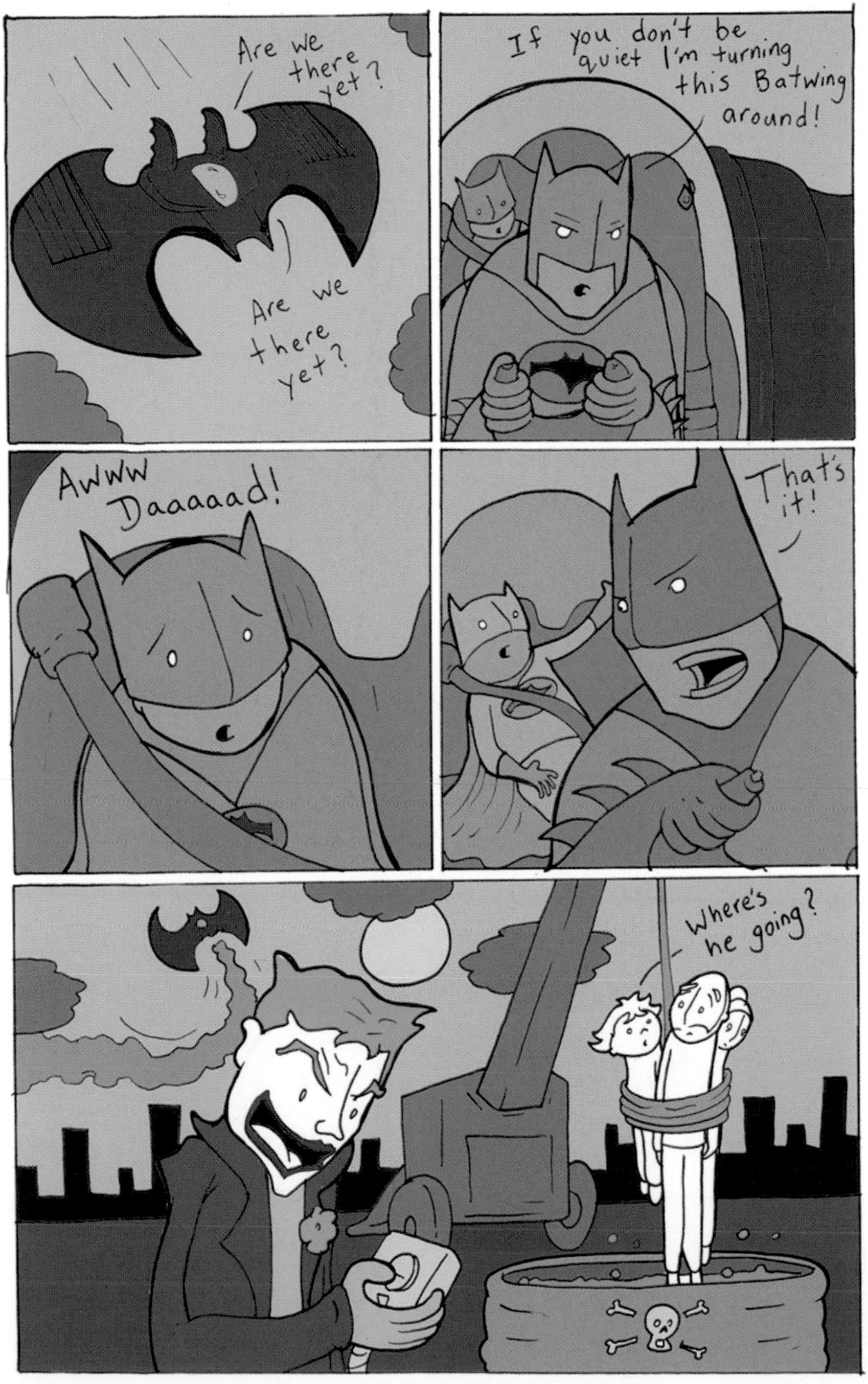
Are we there yet?
Are we there yet?
If you don't be quiet I'm turning this Batwing around!
Awww Daaaaad!
That's it!
Where's he going?

All these stars make me feel small and insignificant.
Wanna flip?

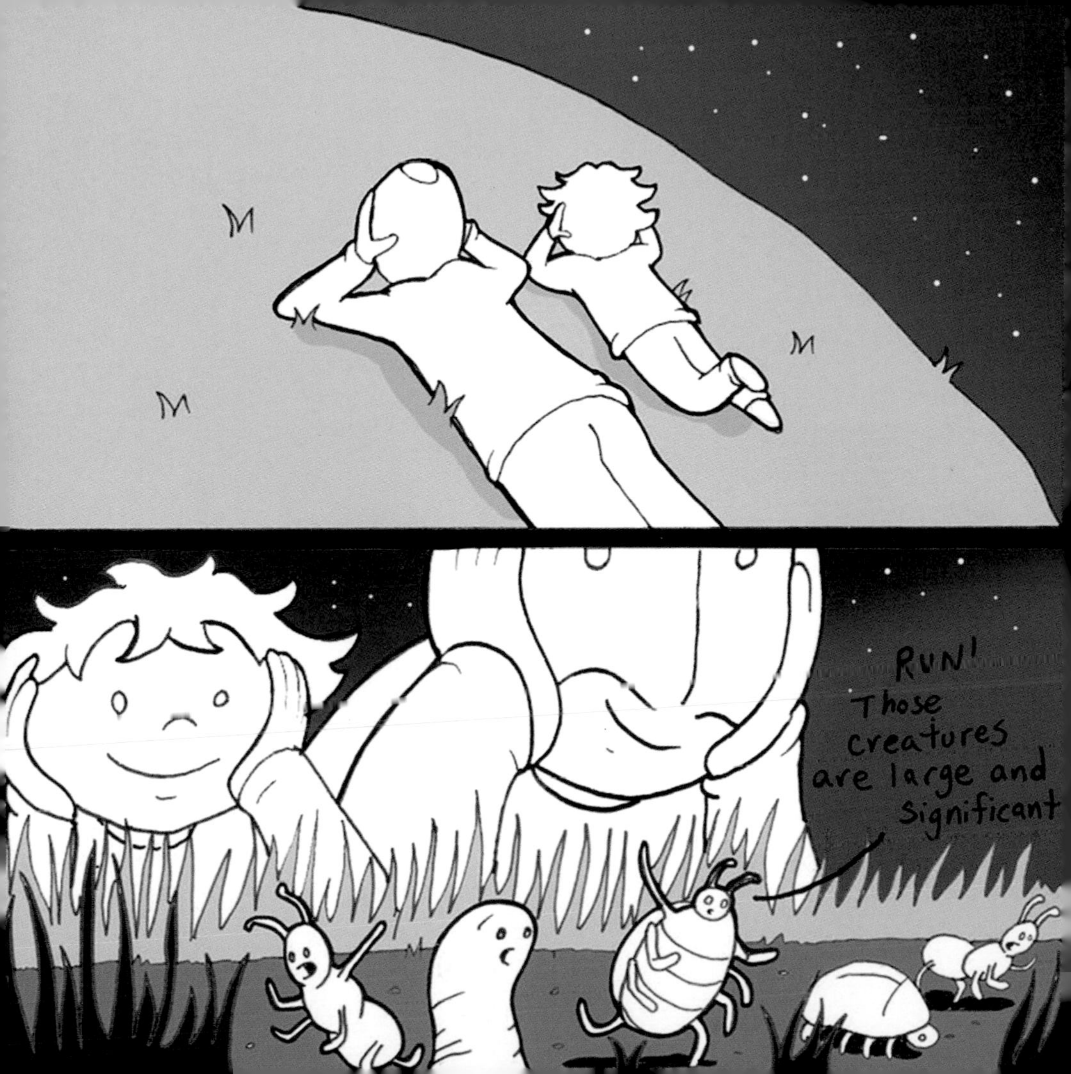
RUN! Those creatures are large and significant

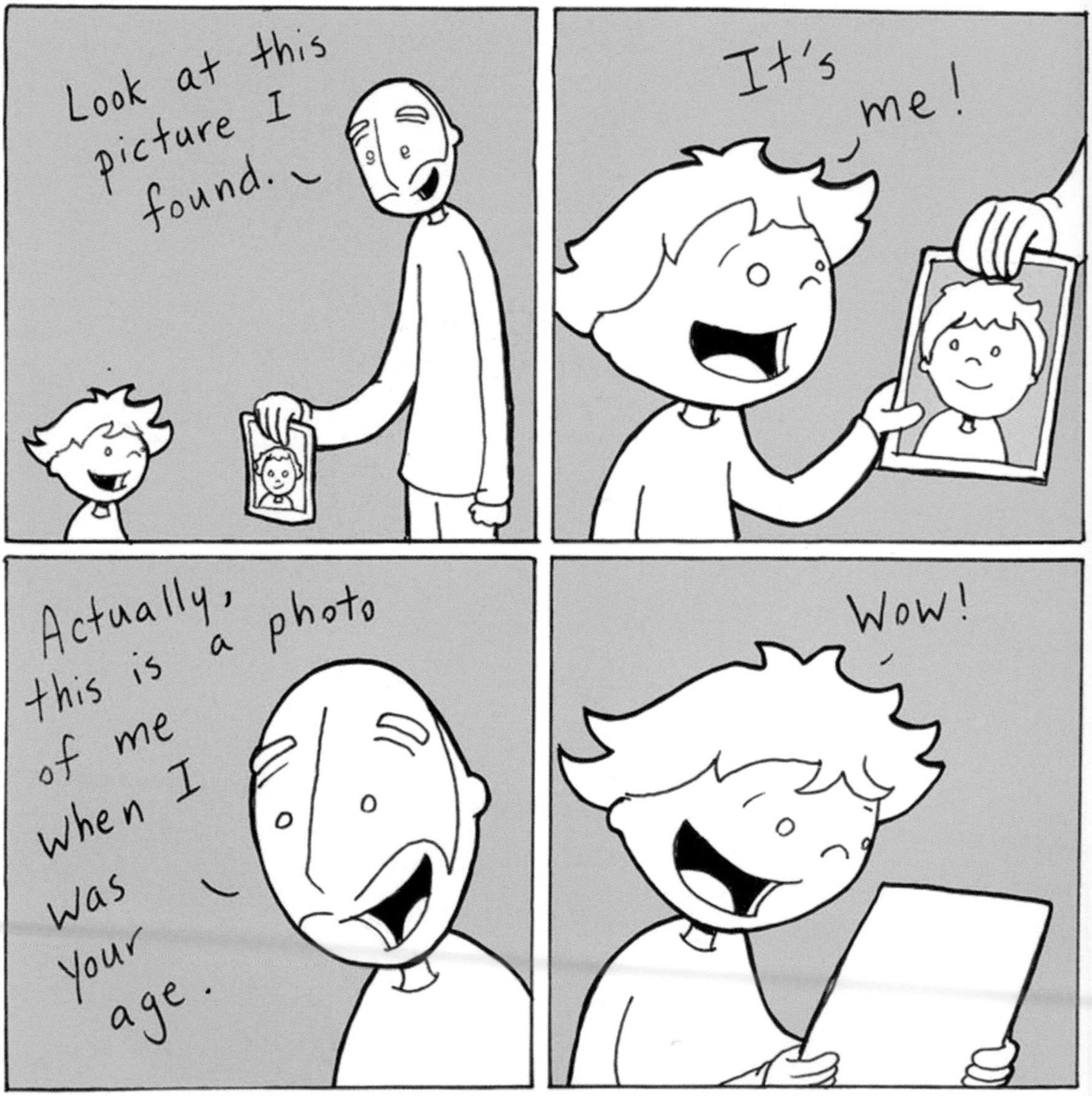
Look at this picture I found.
It's me!
Actually, this is a photo of me when I was your age.
Wow!

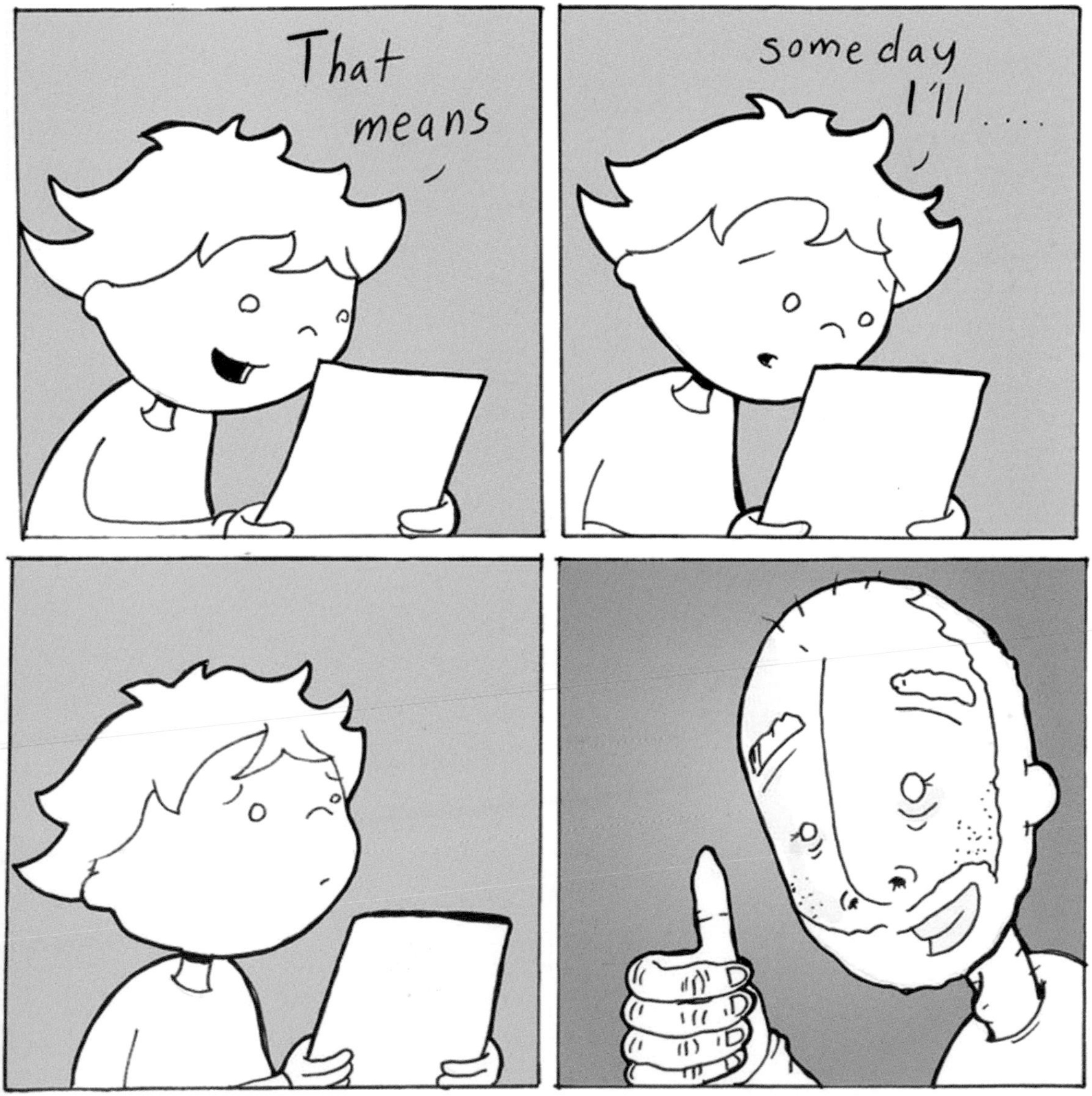
That means
someday I'll....

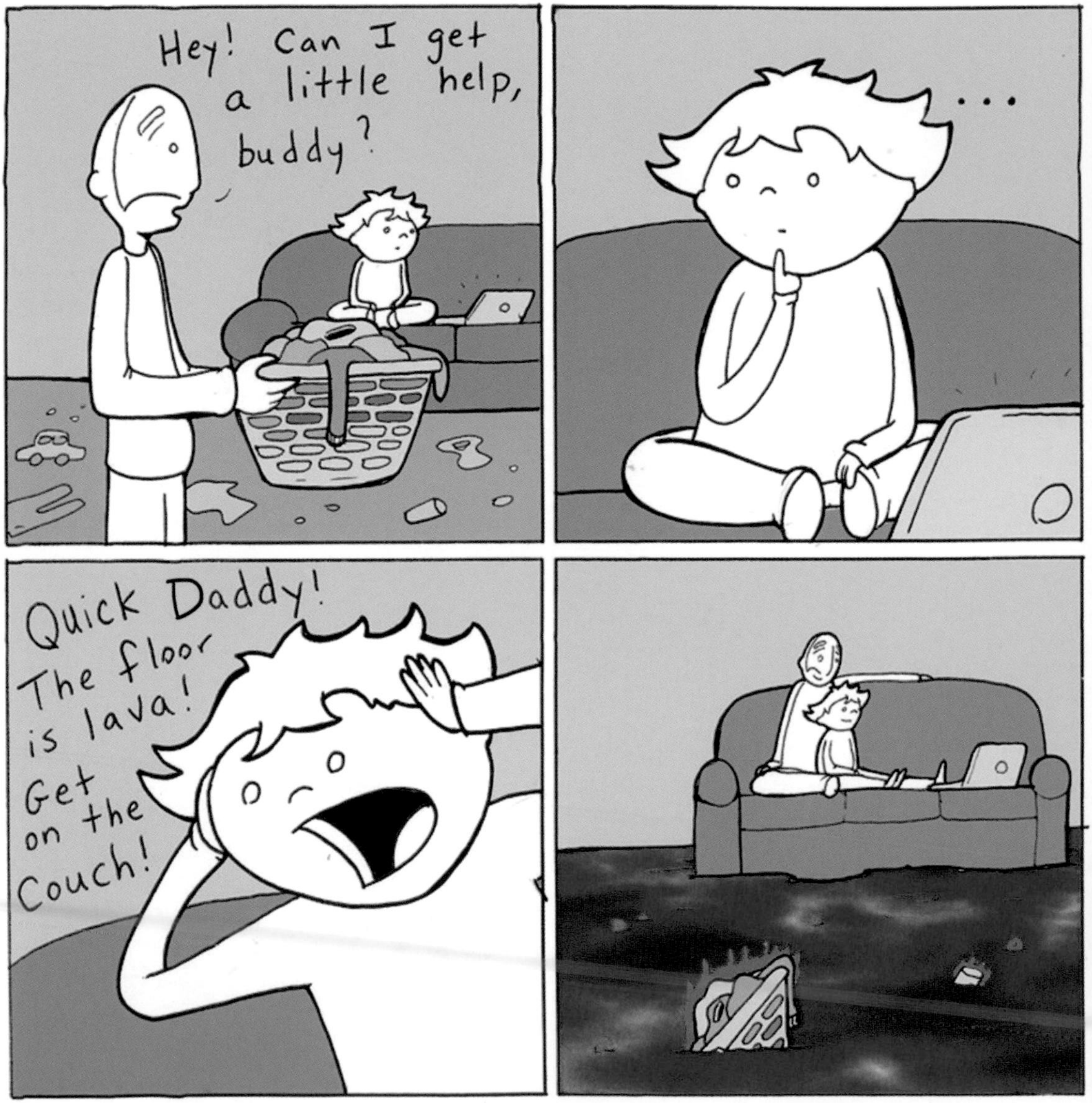
Hey! Can I get a little help, buddy?
...
Quick Daddy! The floor is lava! Get on the Couch!

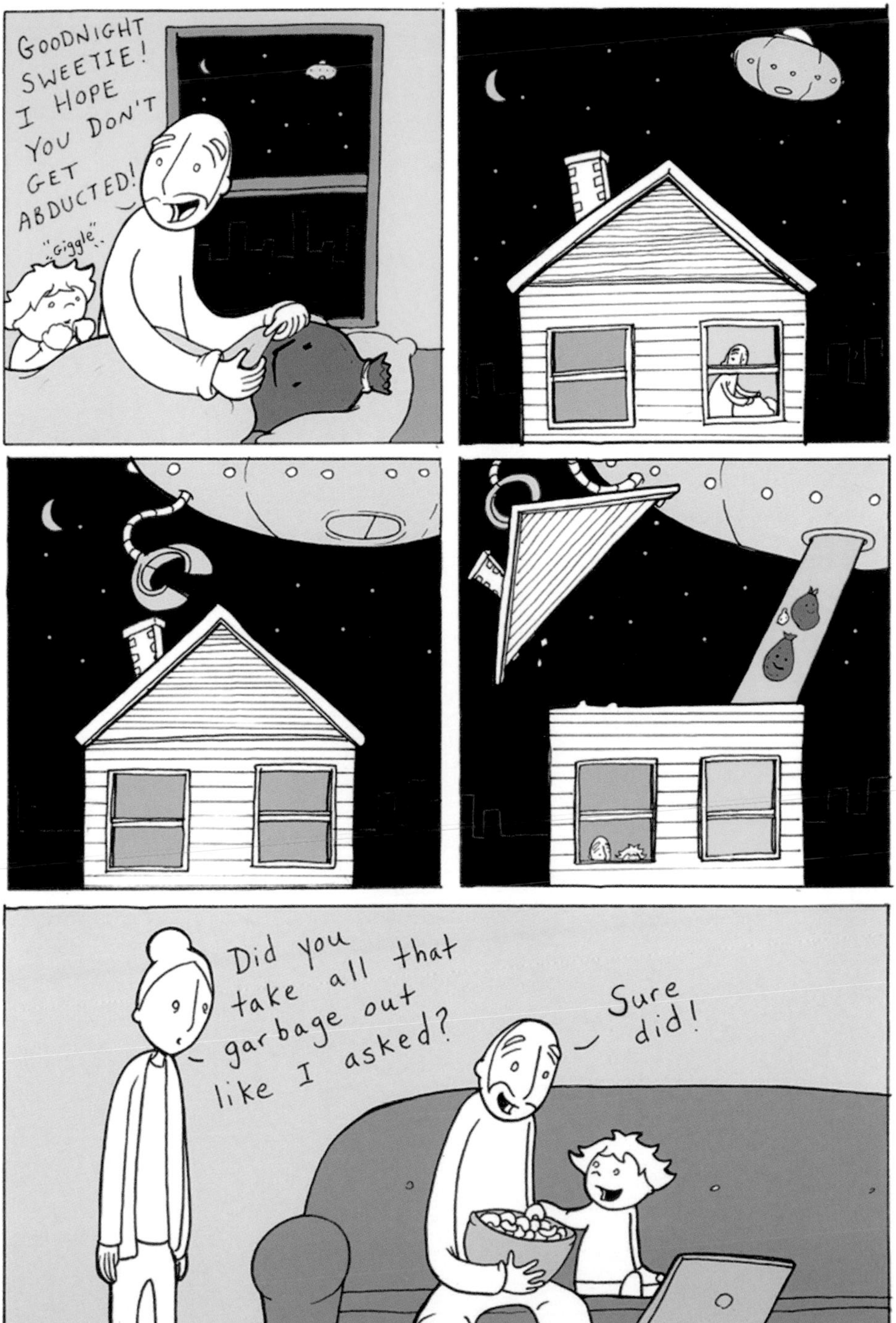
GOODNIGHT SWEETIE! I HOPE YOU DON'T GET ABDUCTED!
"giggle"
Did you take all that garbage out like I asked?
Sure did!

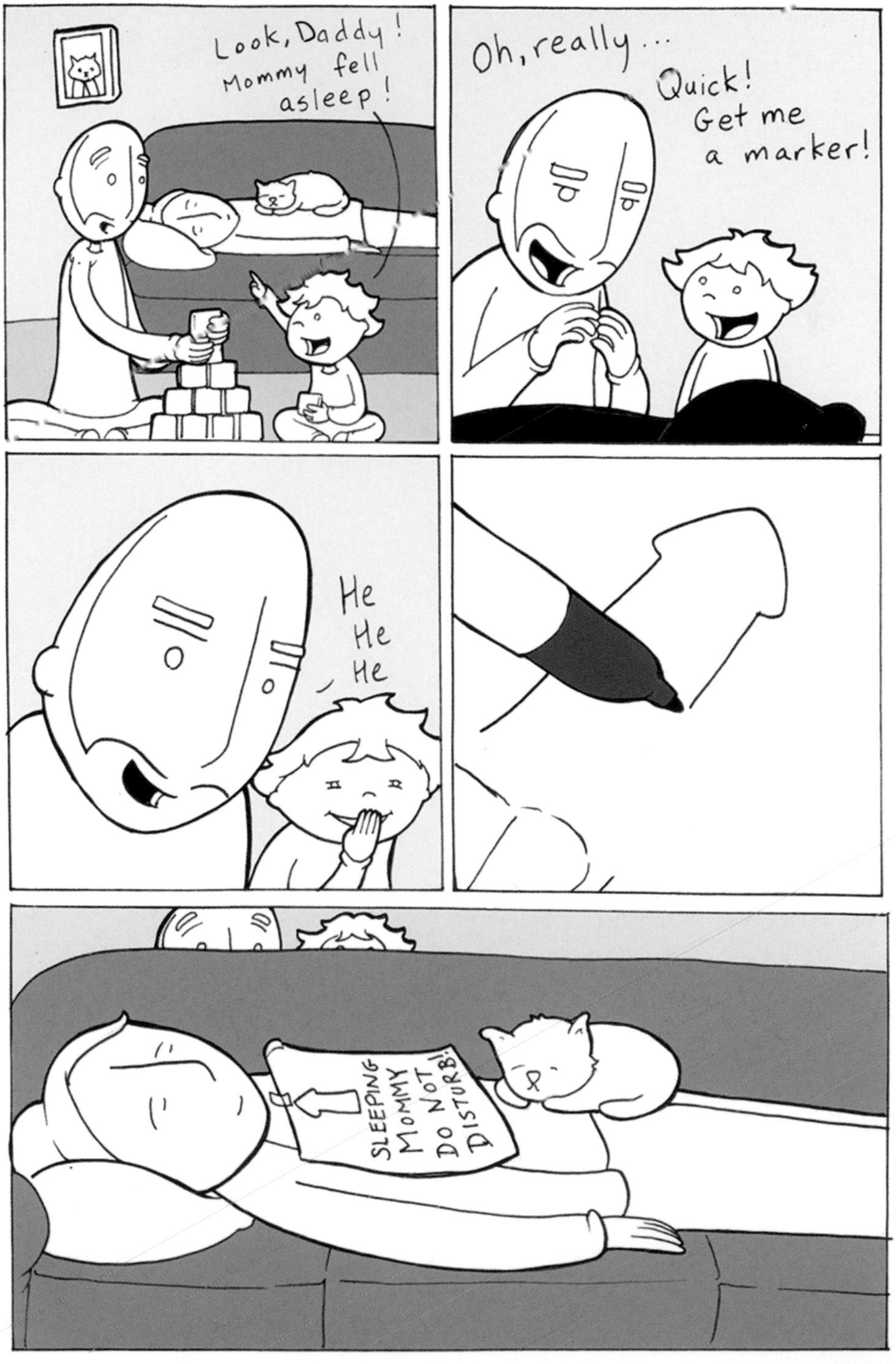
Look, Daddy! Mommy fell asleep!
Oh, really...
Quick! Get me a marker!
He He He
SLEEPING MOMMY DO NOT DISTURB!

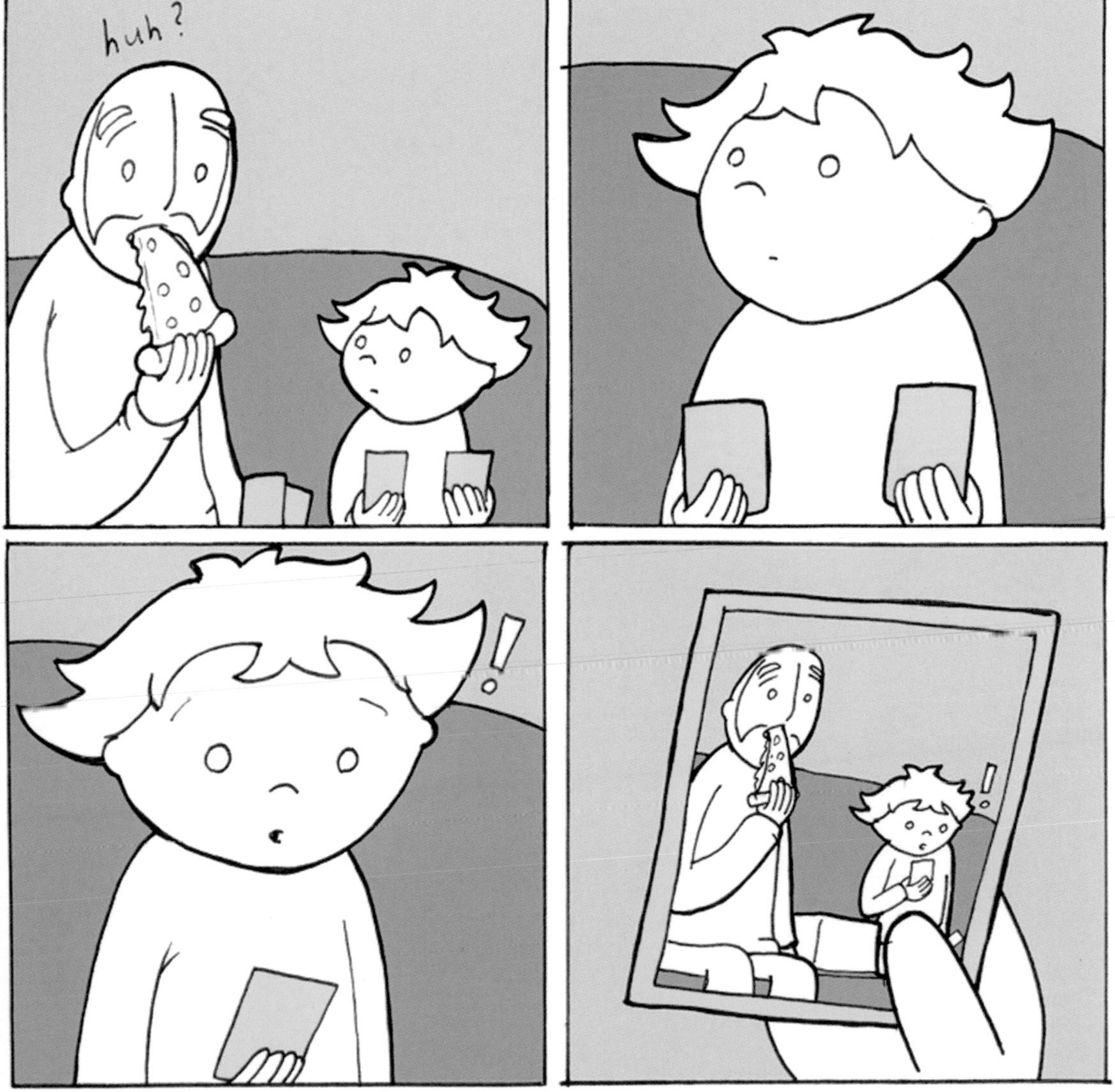
huh?
!
!

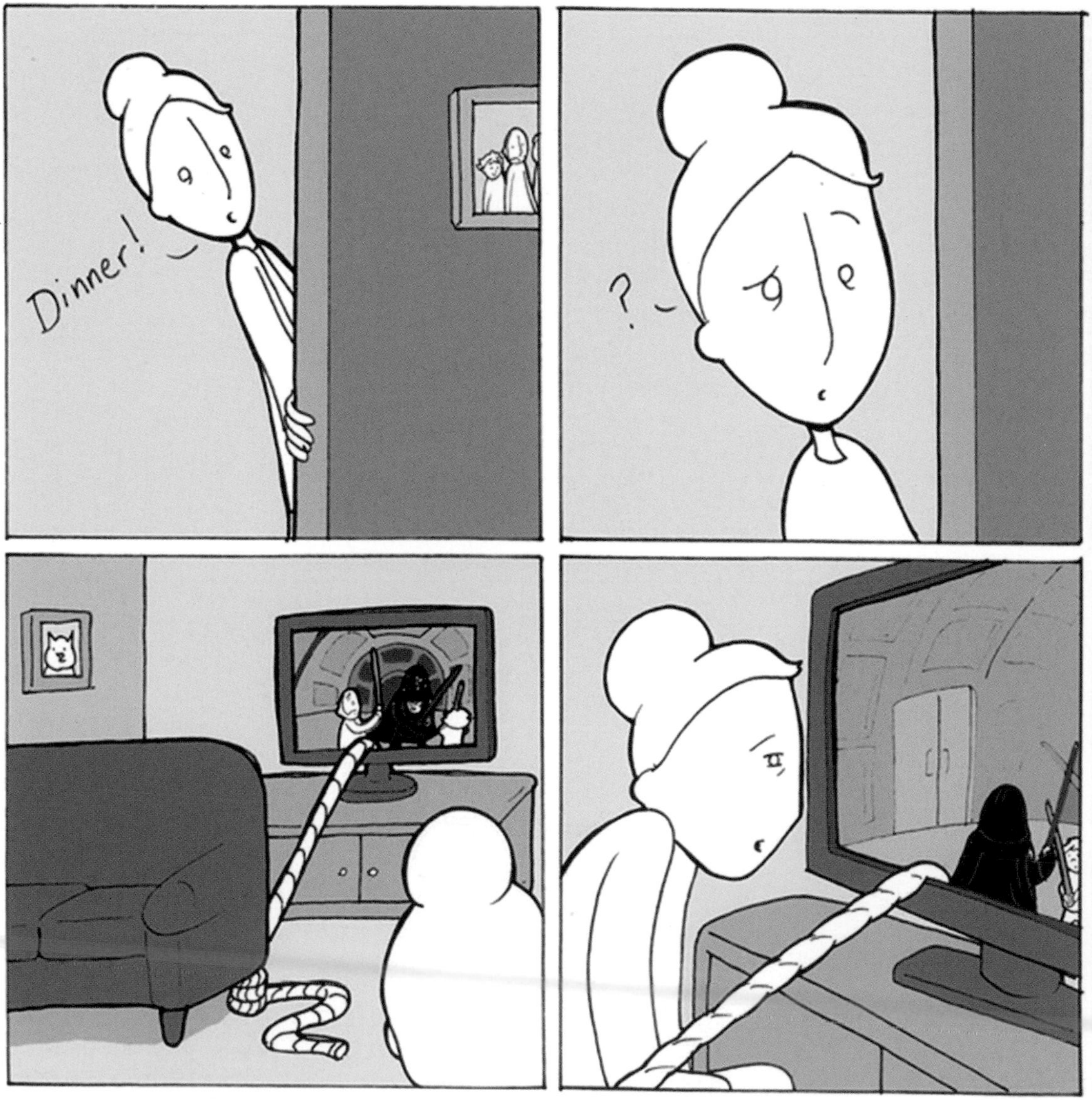
Dinner!
?

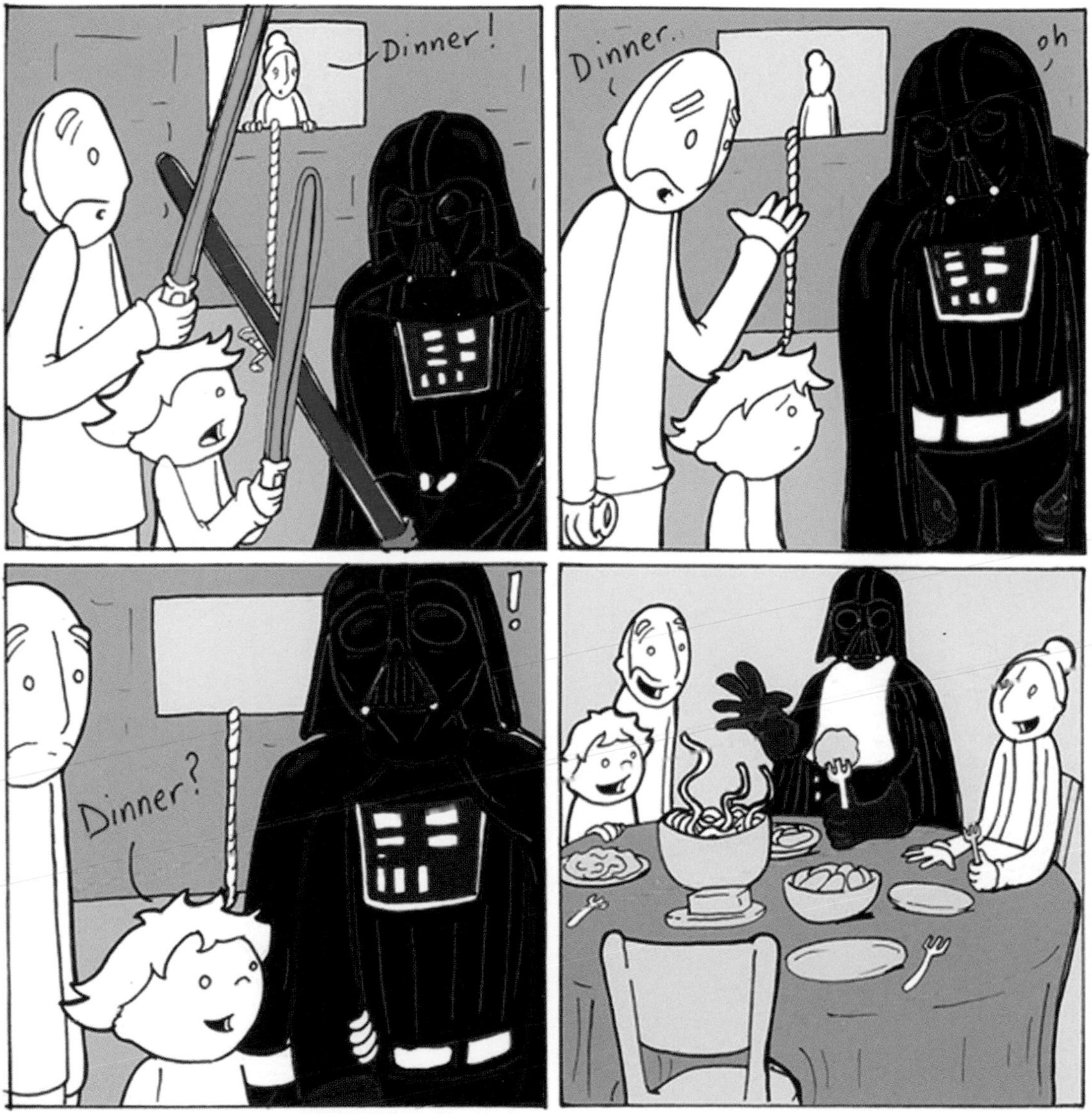
Dinner!
Dinner.
oh
!
Dinner?

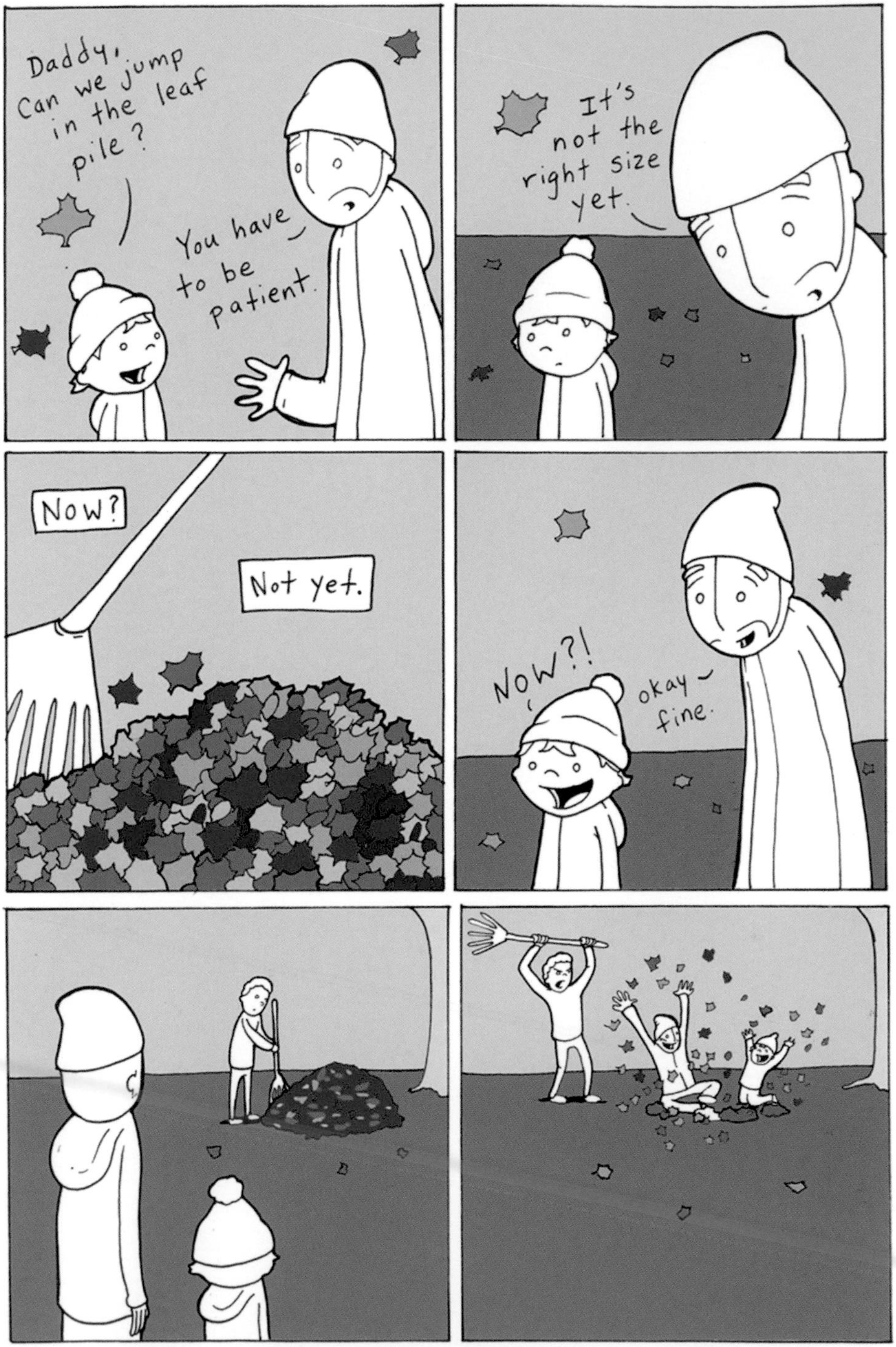
Daddy, Can we jump in the leaf pile?
You have to be patient.
It's not the right size yet.
Now?
Not yet.
Now?!
okay fine.

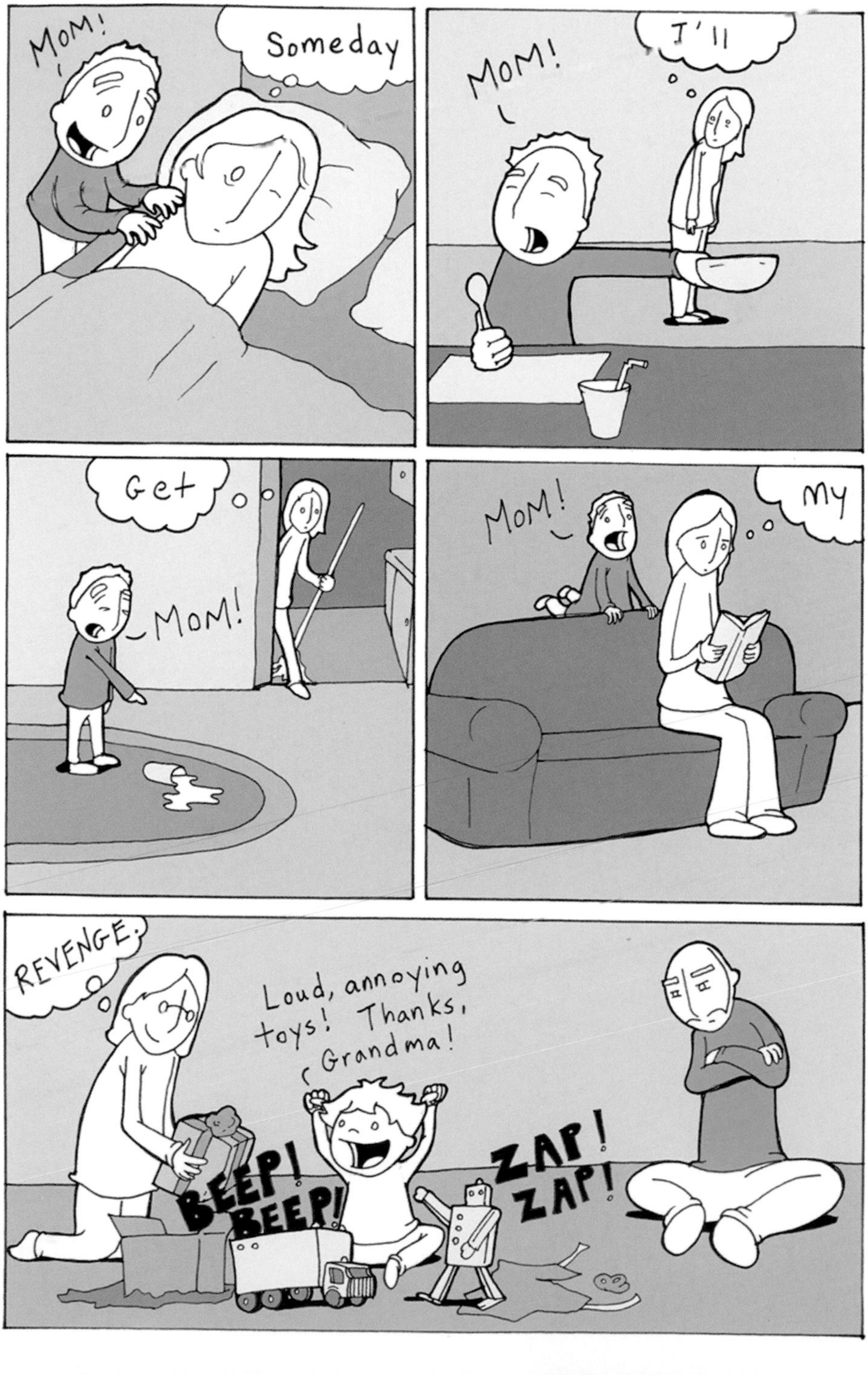
MOM!
Someday
MOM!
I'll
Get
MOM!
MOM!
my
REVENGE.
Loud, annoying toys! Thanks, Grandma!
BEEP! BEEP!
ZAP! ZAP!

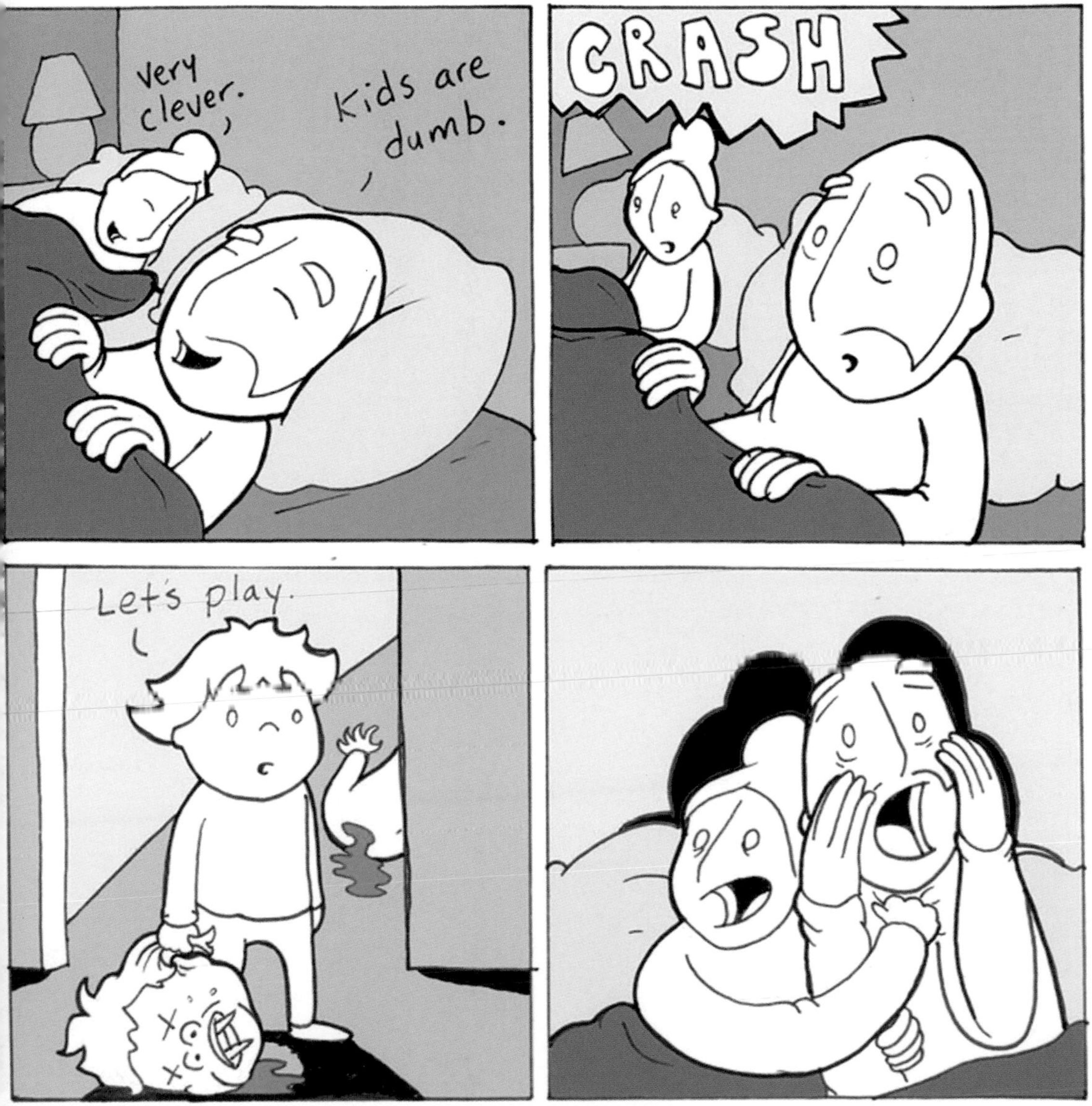

Very clever.
Kids are dumb.
CRASH
Let's play.

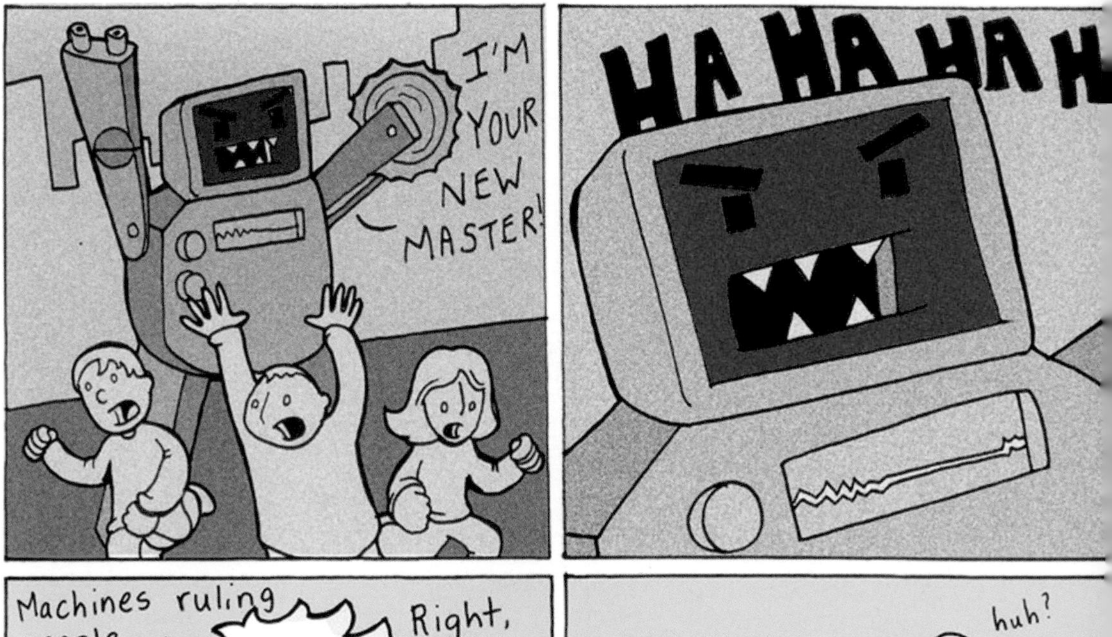
I'M YOUR NEW MASTER!
HA HA HA HA H
Machines ruling people... That's dumb.
Right, Mom and Dad?
huh?

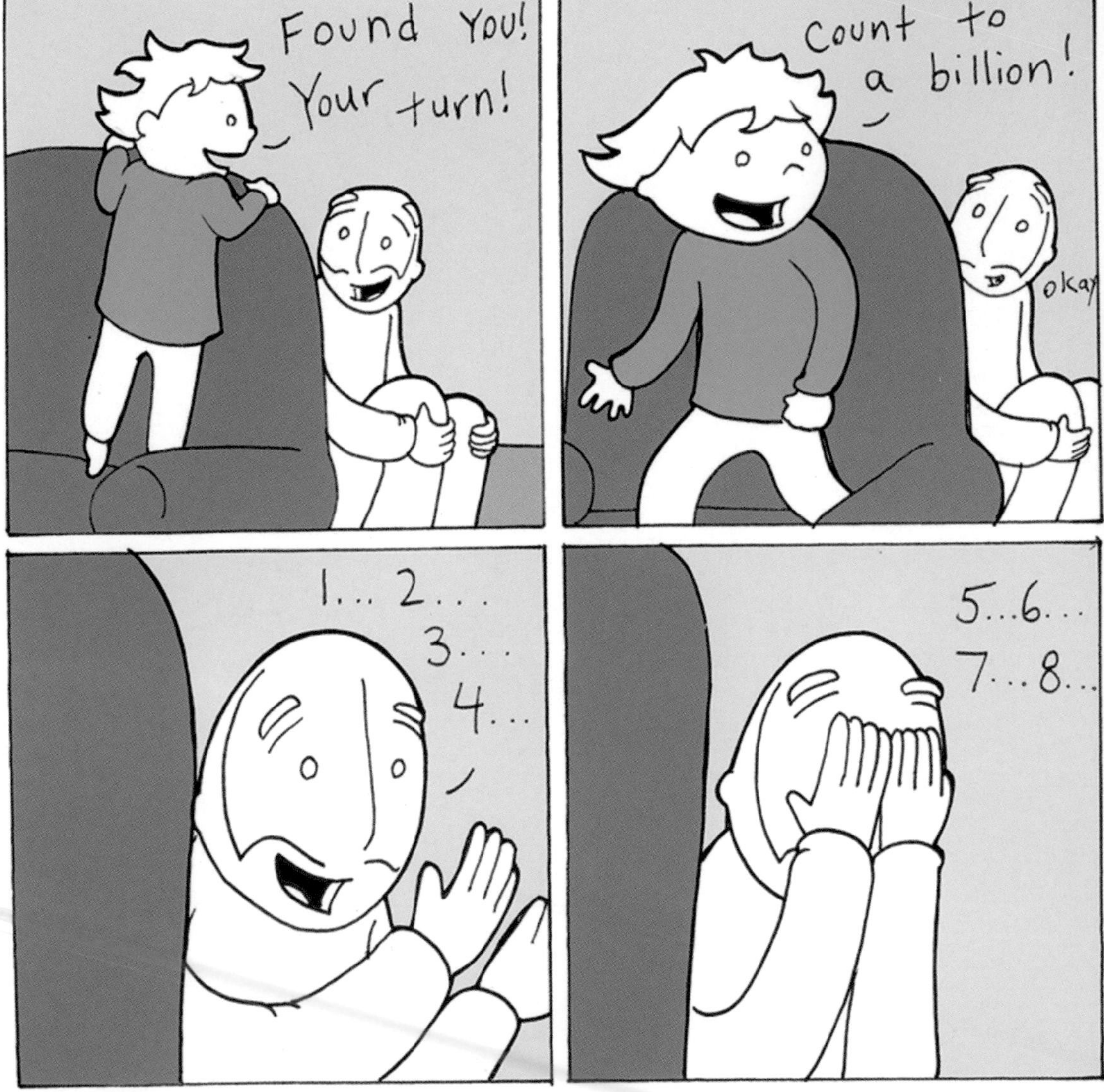
Found You! Your turn!
Count to a billion!
okay
1... 2...
3...
4...
5...6...
7...8...

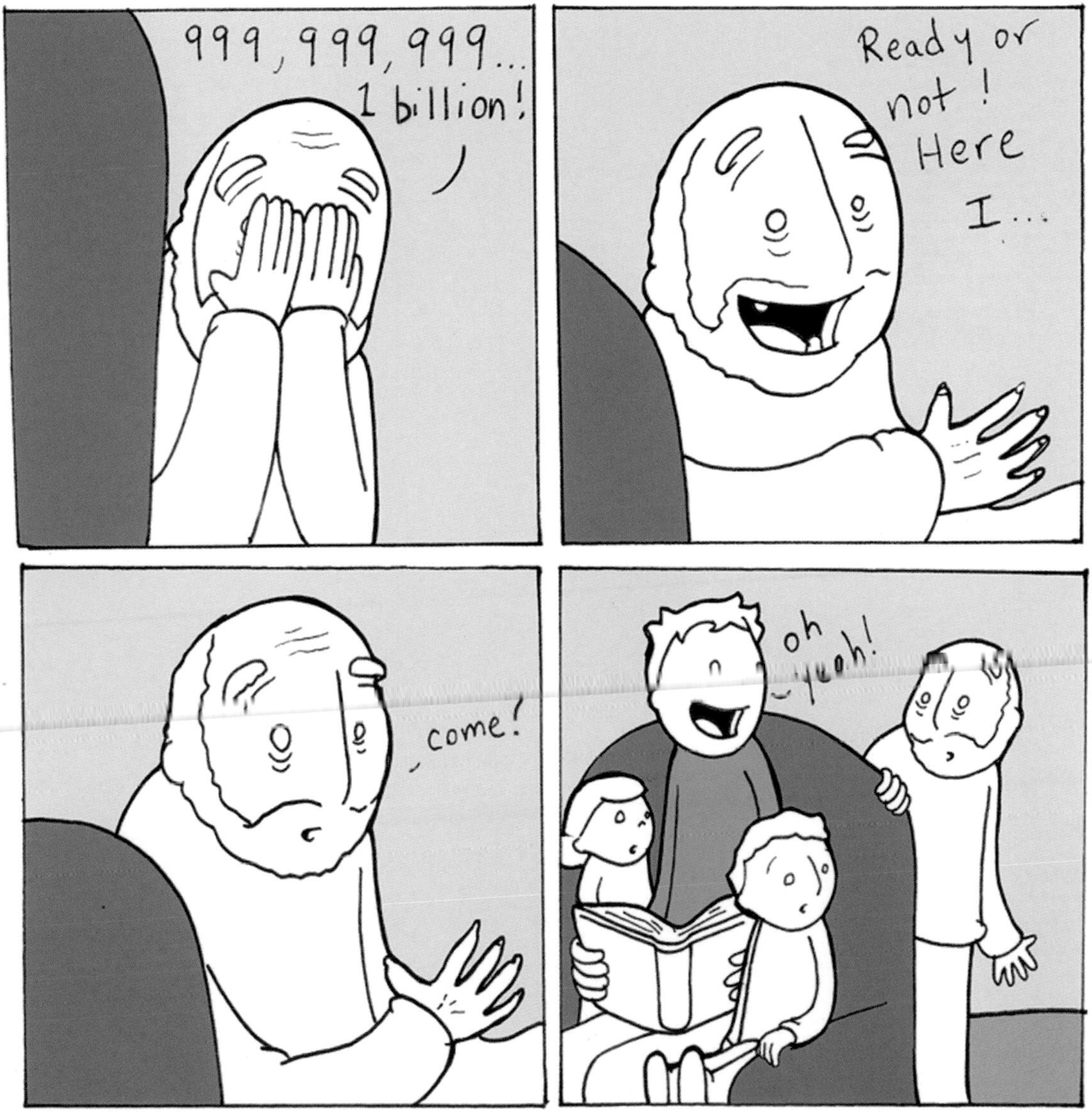
999,999,999...
1 billion!
Ready or
not! Here
I...
come!
oh
yeah!

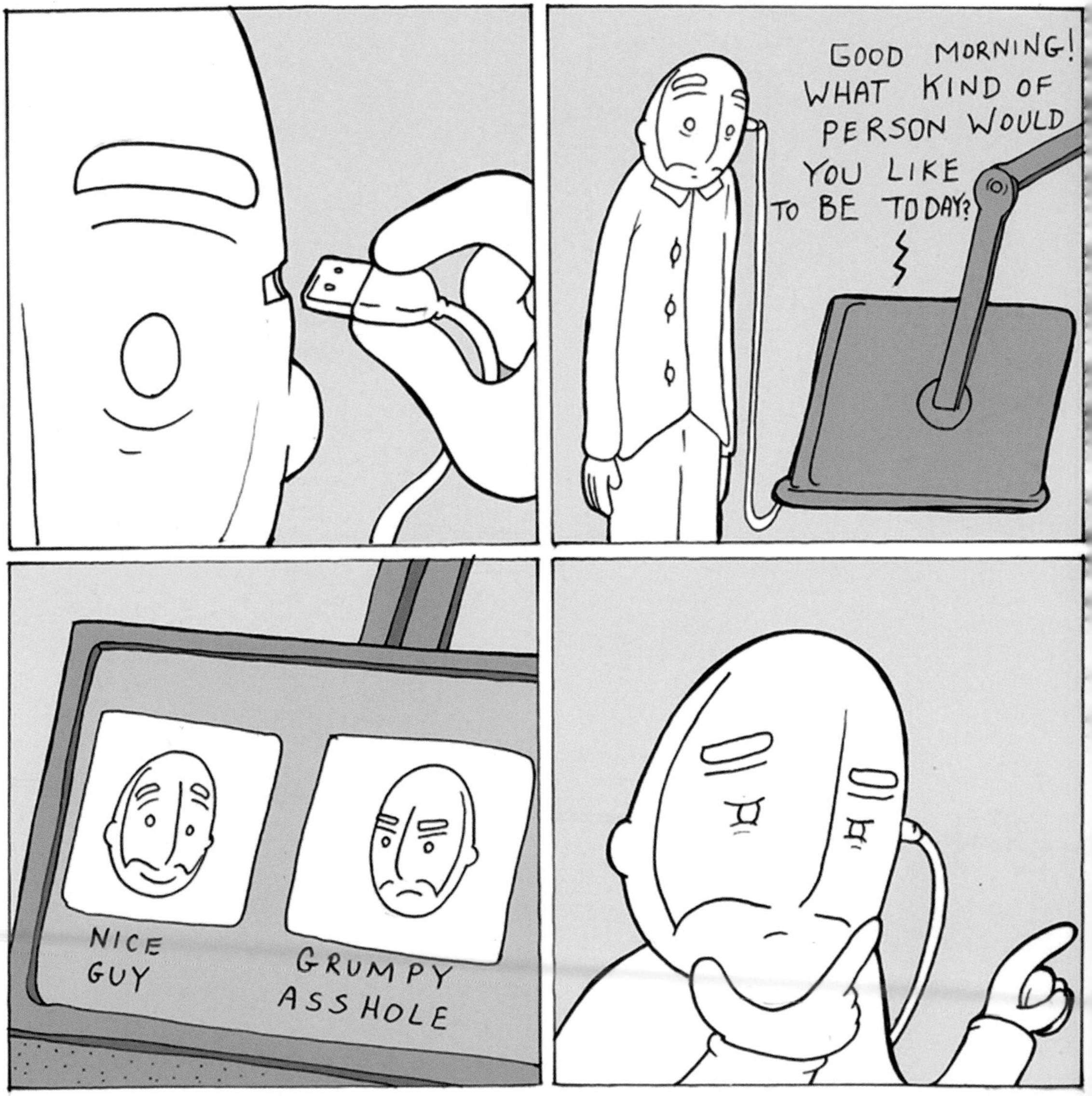
GOOD MORNING! WHAT KIND OF PERSON WOULD YOU LIKE TO BE TODAY?
NICE GUY
GRUMPY ASSHOLE

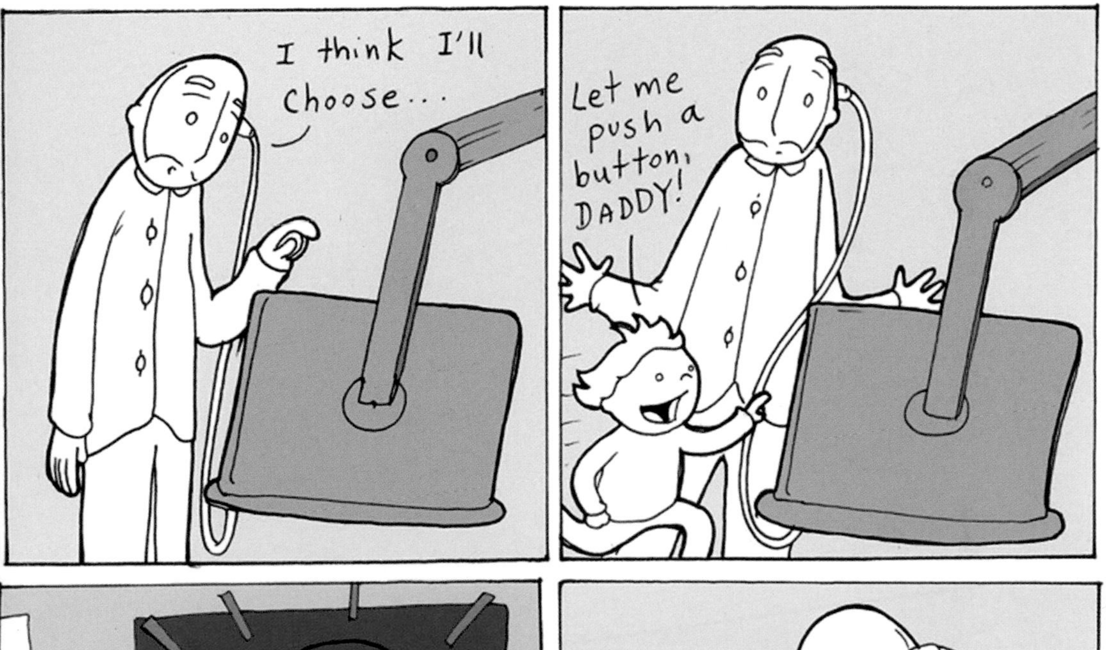
I think I'll choose...
Let me push a button, DADDY!
UMPY
SS HOLE

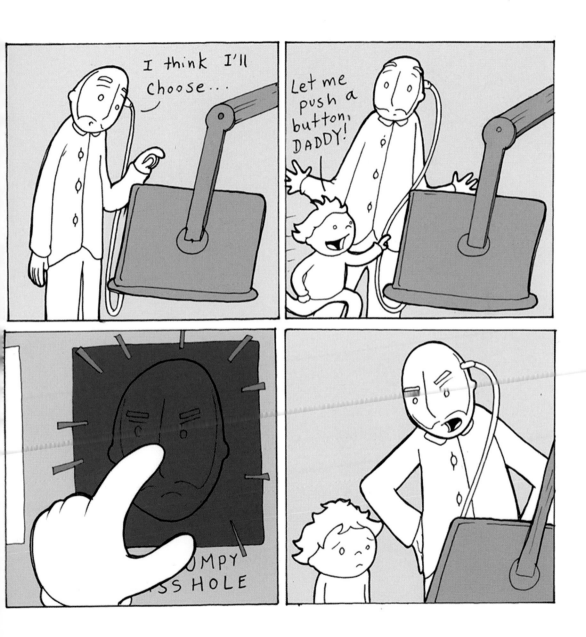

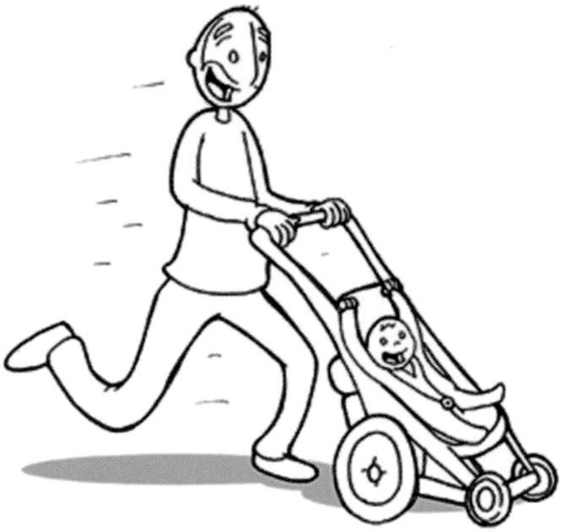

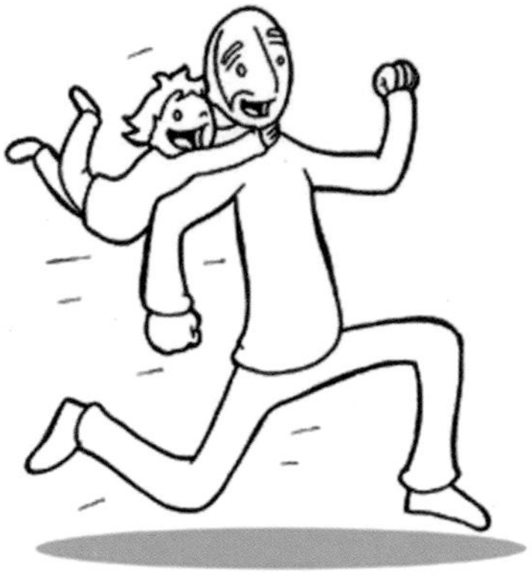

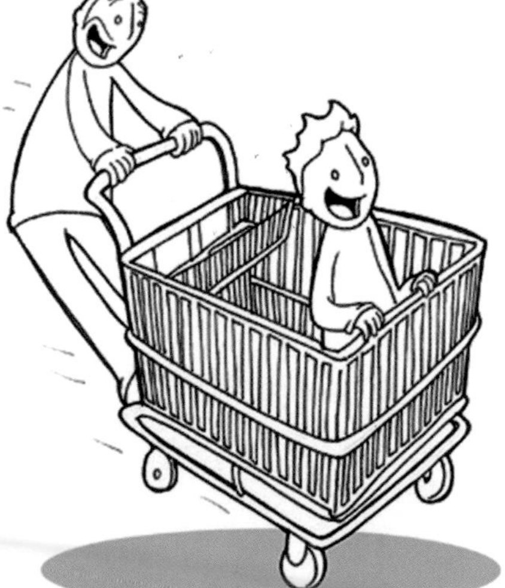

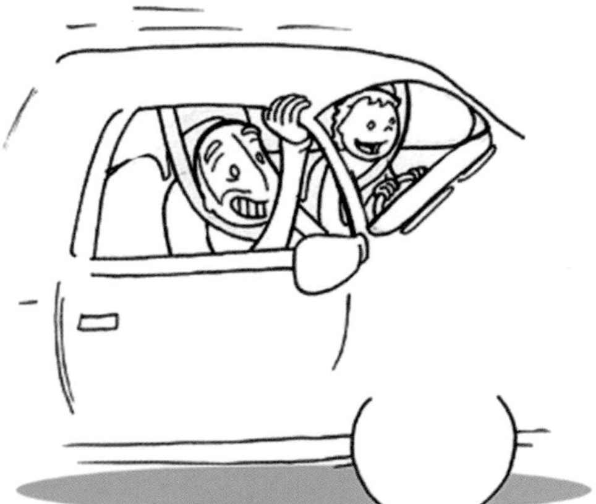

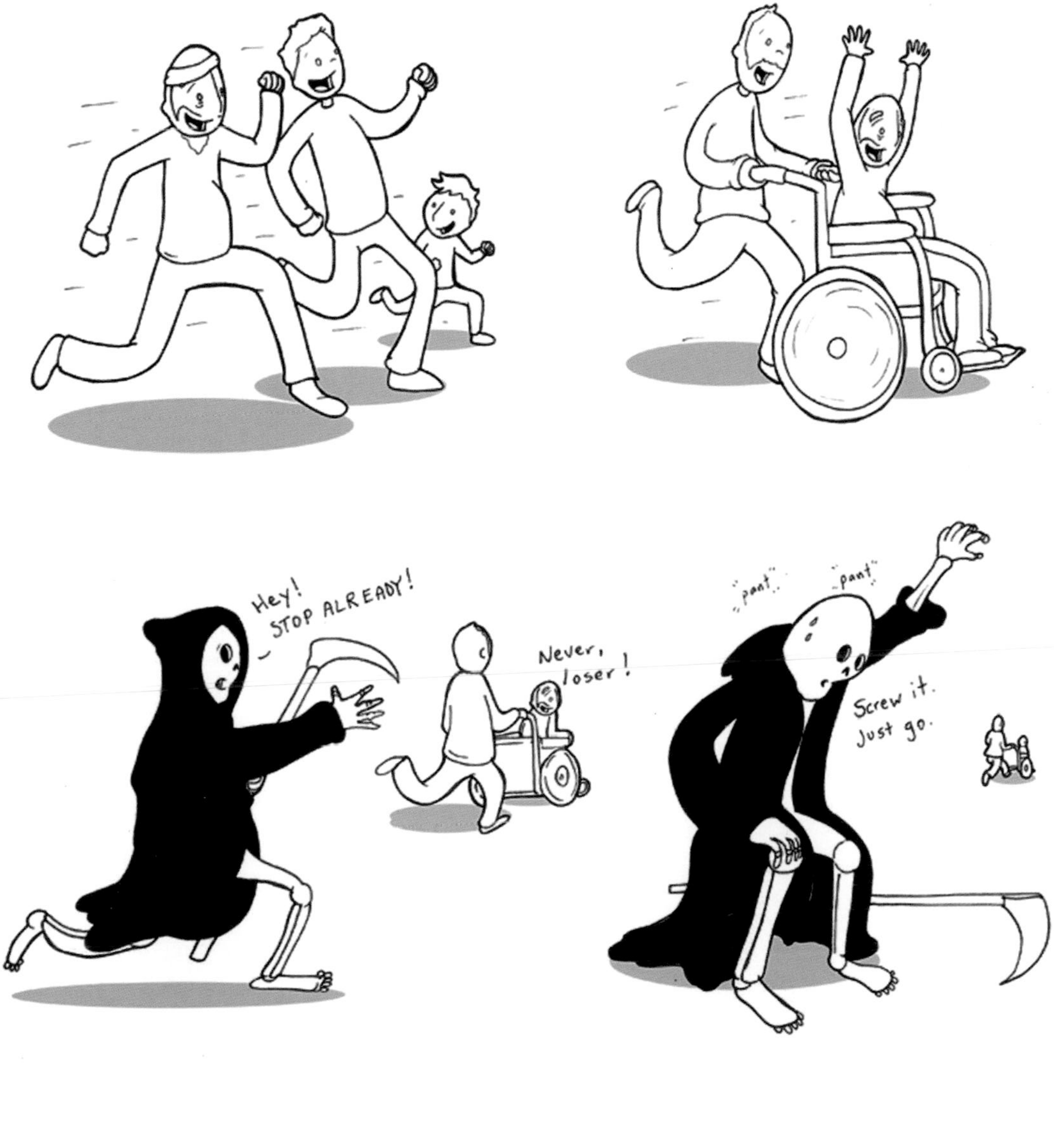
Hey!
STOP ALREADY!
Never, loser!
"pant"
"pant"
Screw it.
Just go.

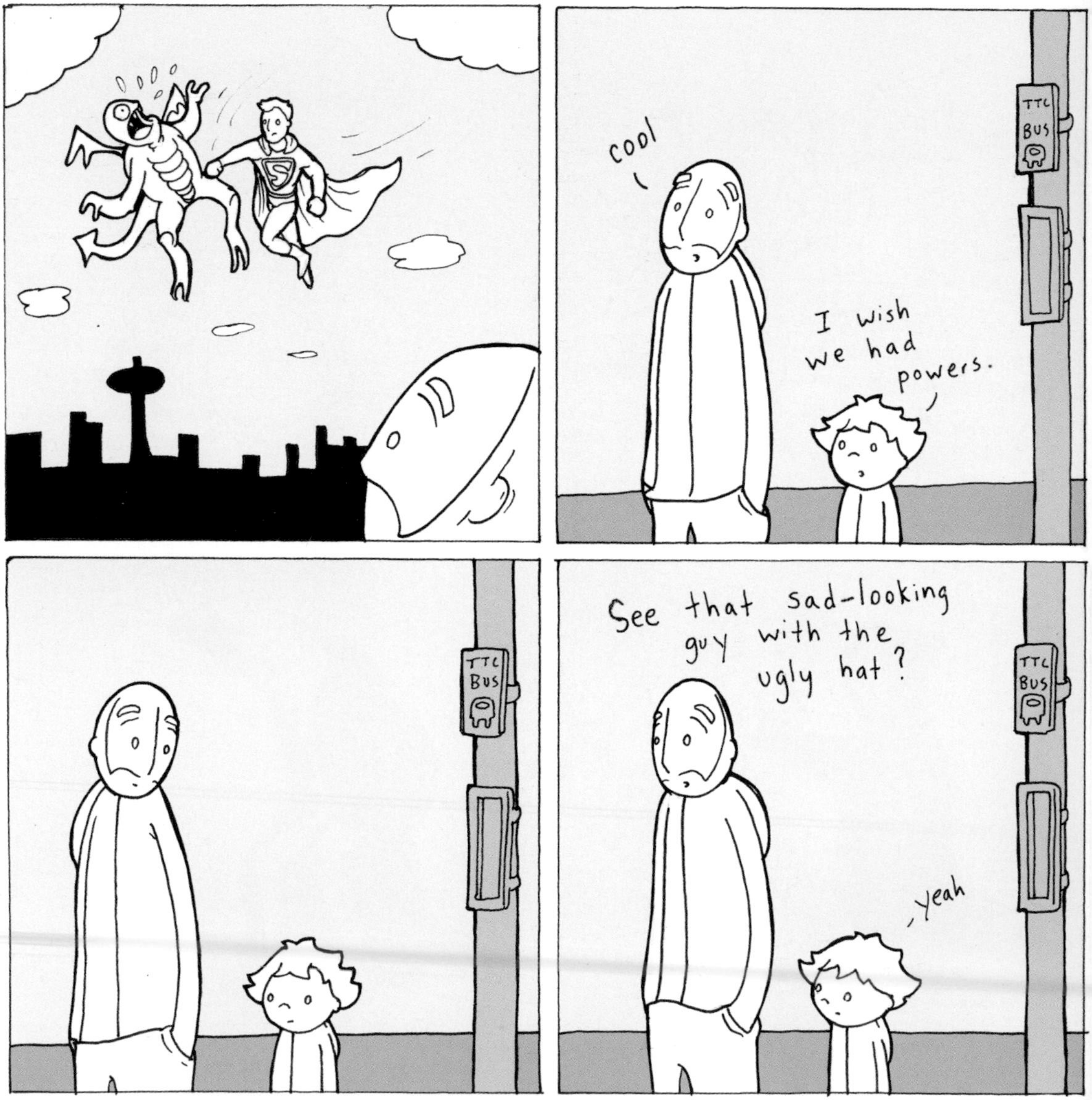
TTC BUS
cool
I wish we had powers.
See that sad-looking guy with the ugly hat?
yeah

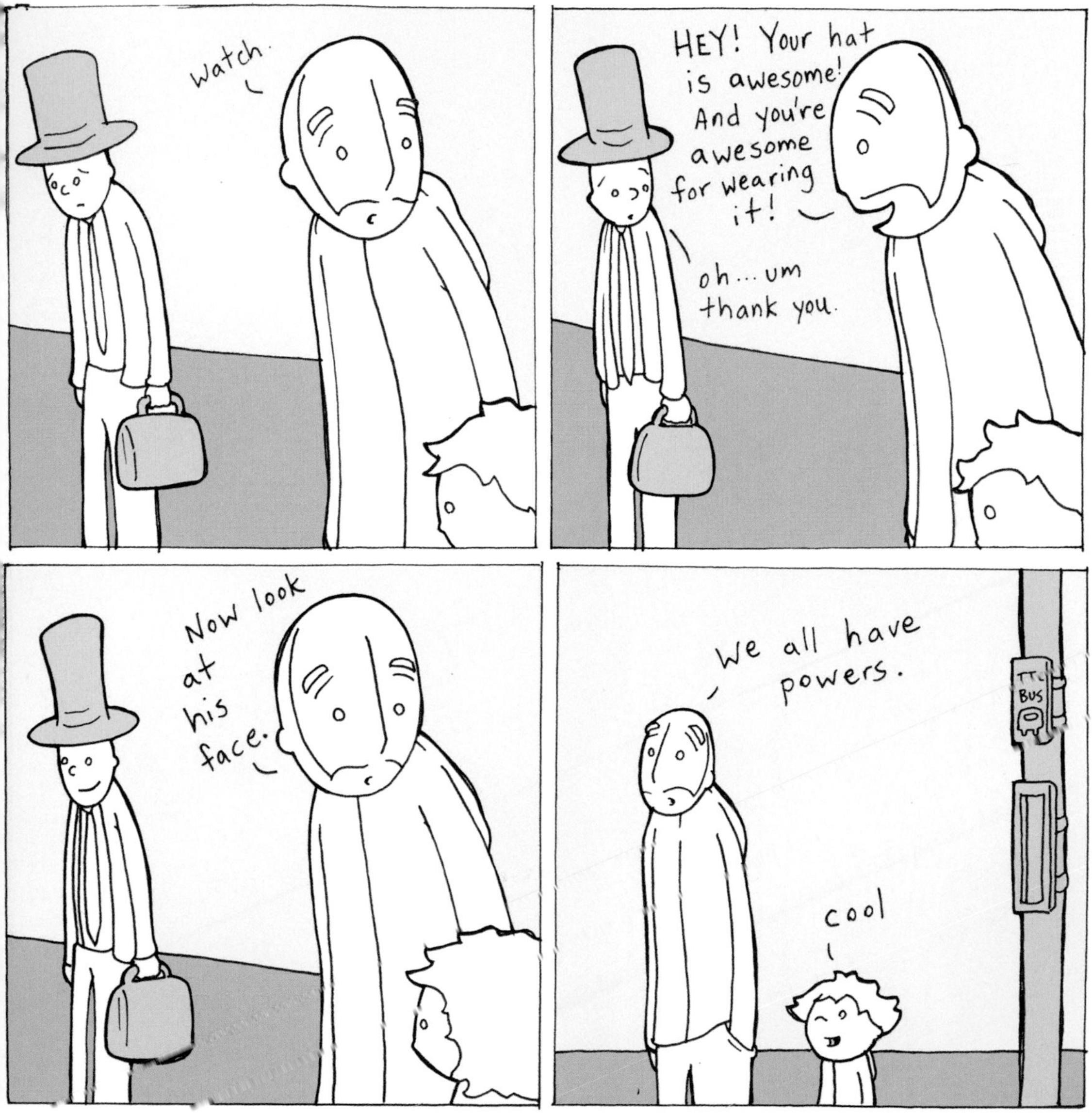
watch.
HEY! Your hat is awesome! And you're awesome for wearing it!
oh... um thank you.
Now look at his face.
We all have powers.
TTC BUS
cool

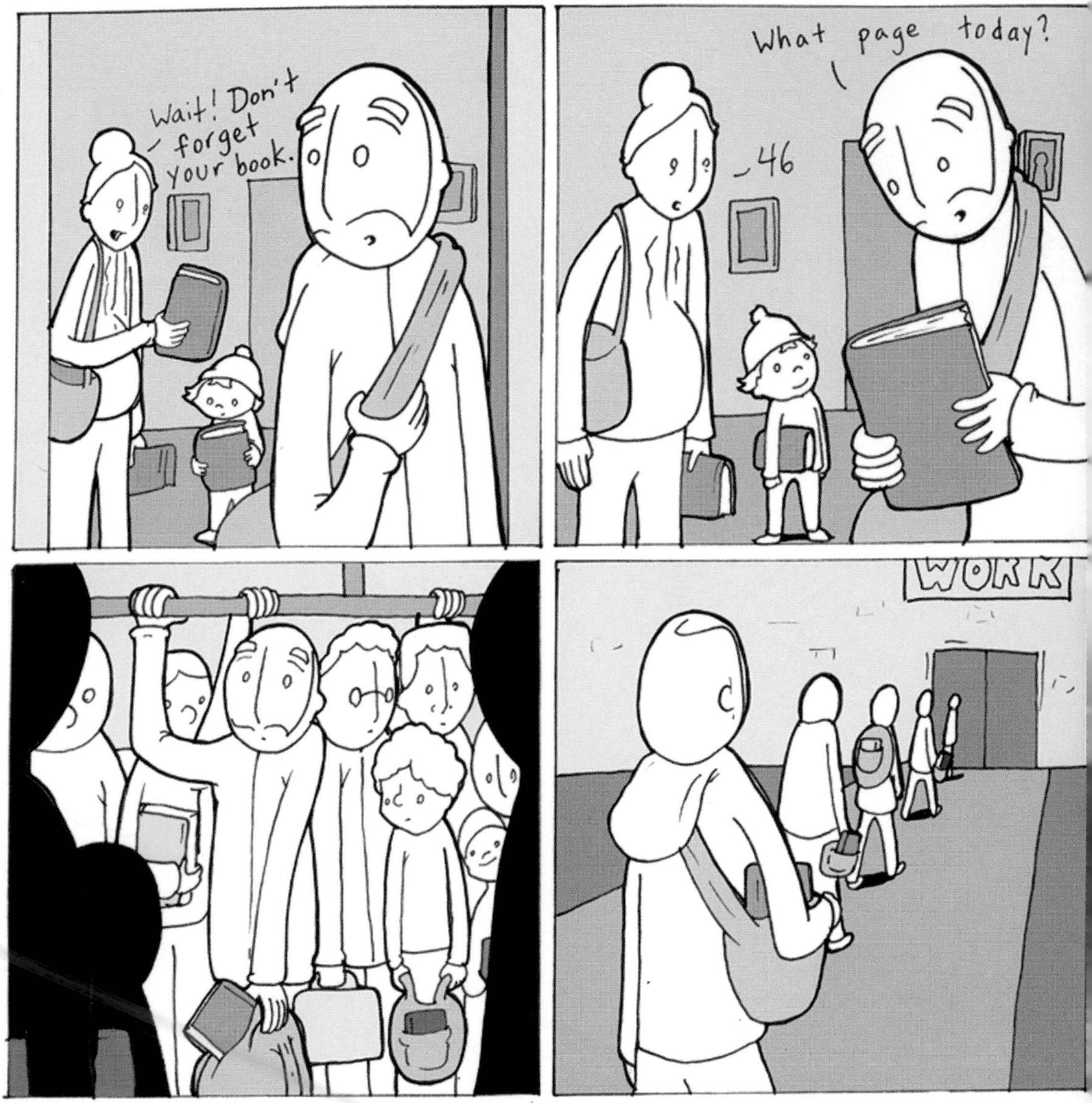
Wait! Don't forget your book.
What page today?
46
WORK

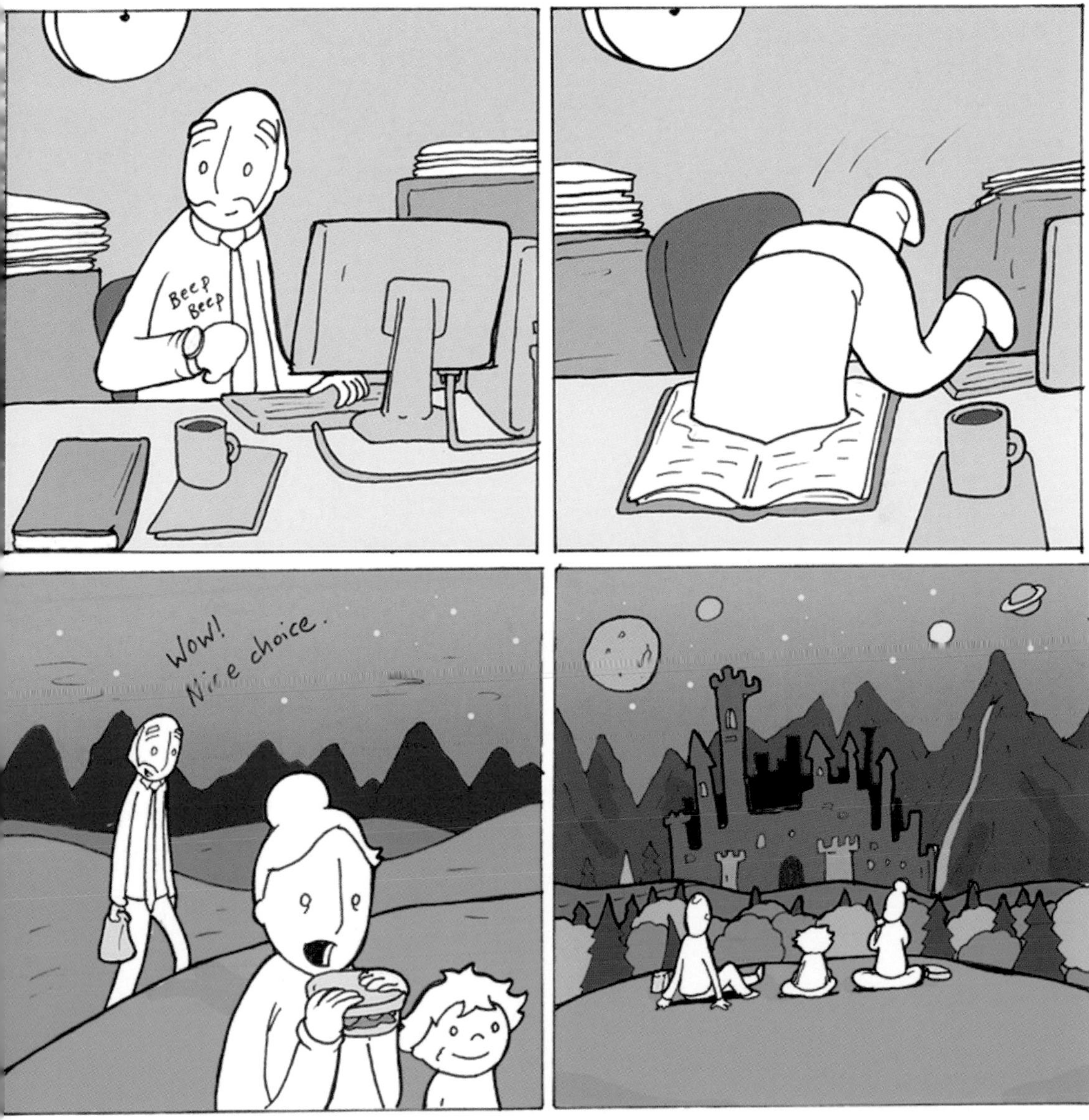
Beep
Beep
Wow!
Nice choice.

79

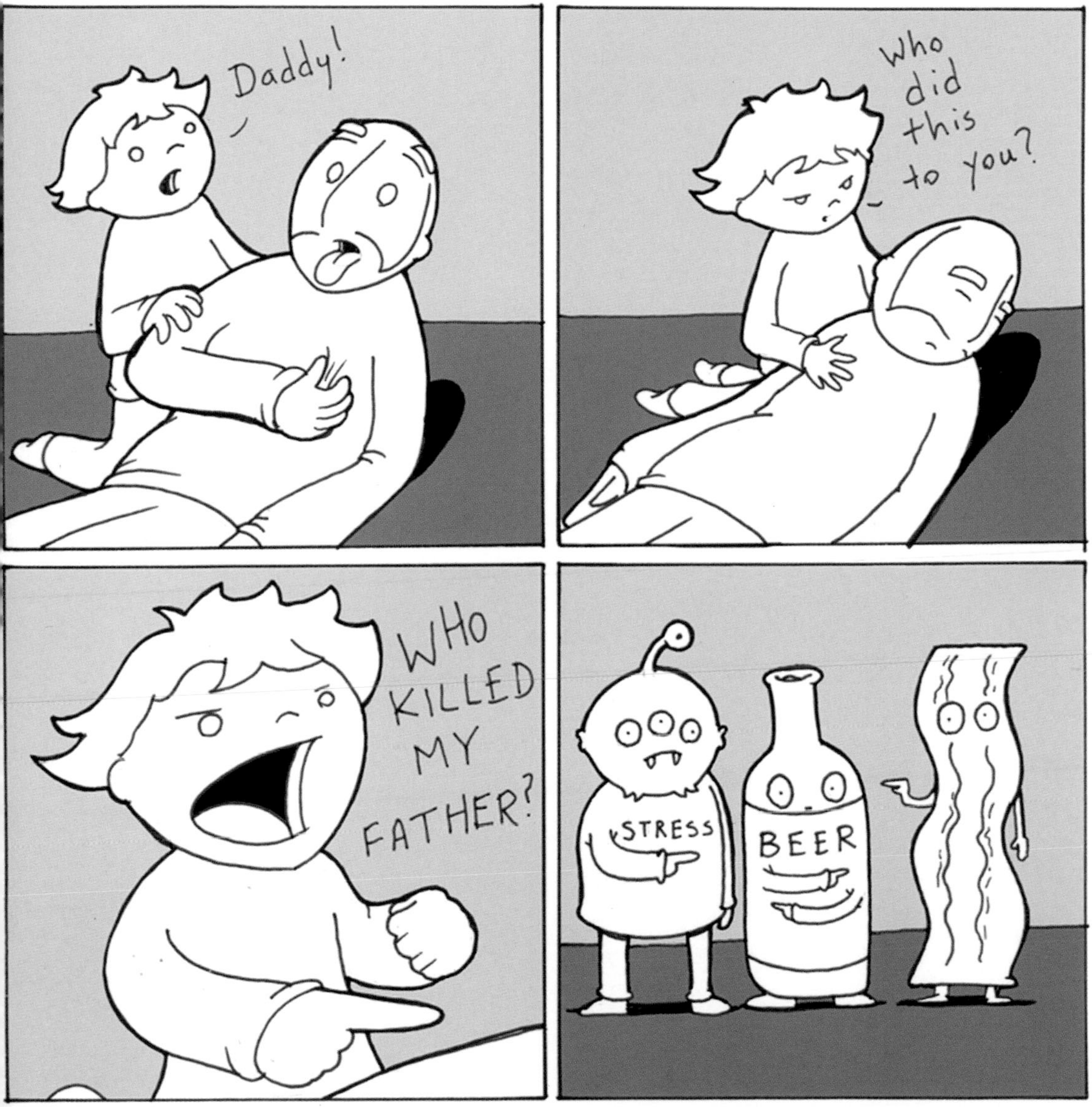
Daddy!
Who did this to you?
WHO KILLED MY FATHER?
STRESS
BEER

85

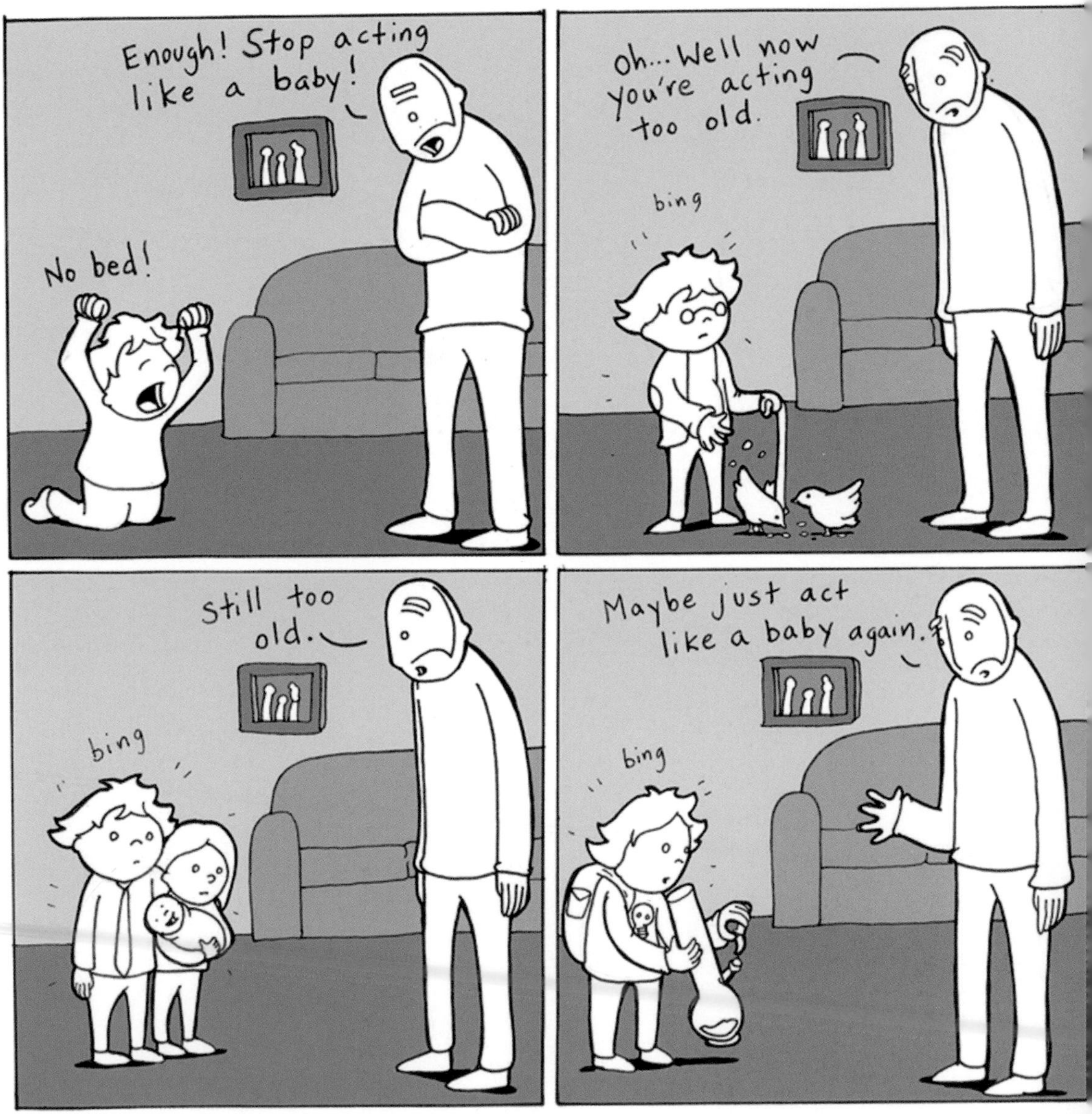
Enough! Stop acting like a baby!
No bed!
Oh... Well now you're acting too old.
bing
Still too old.
bing
Maybe just act like a baby again.
bing

87

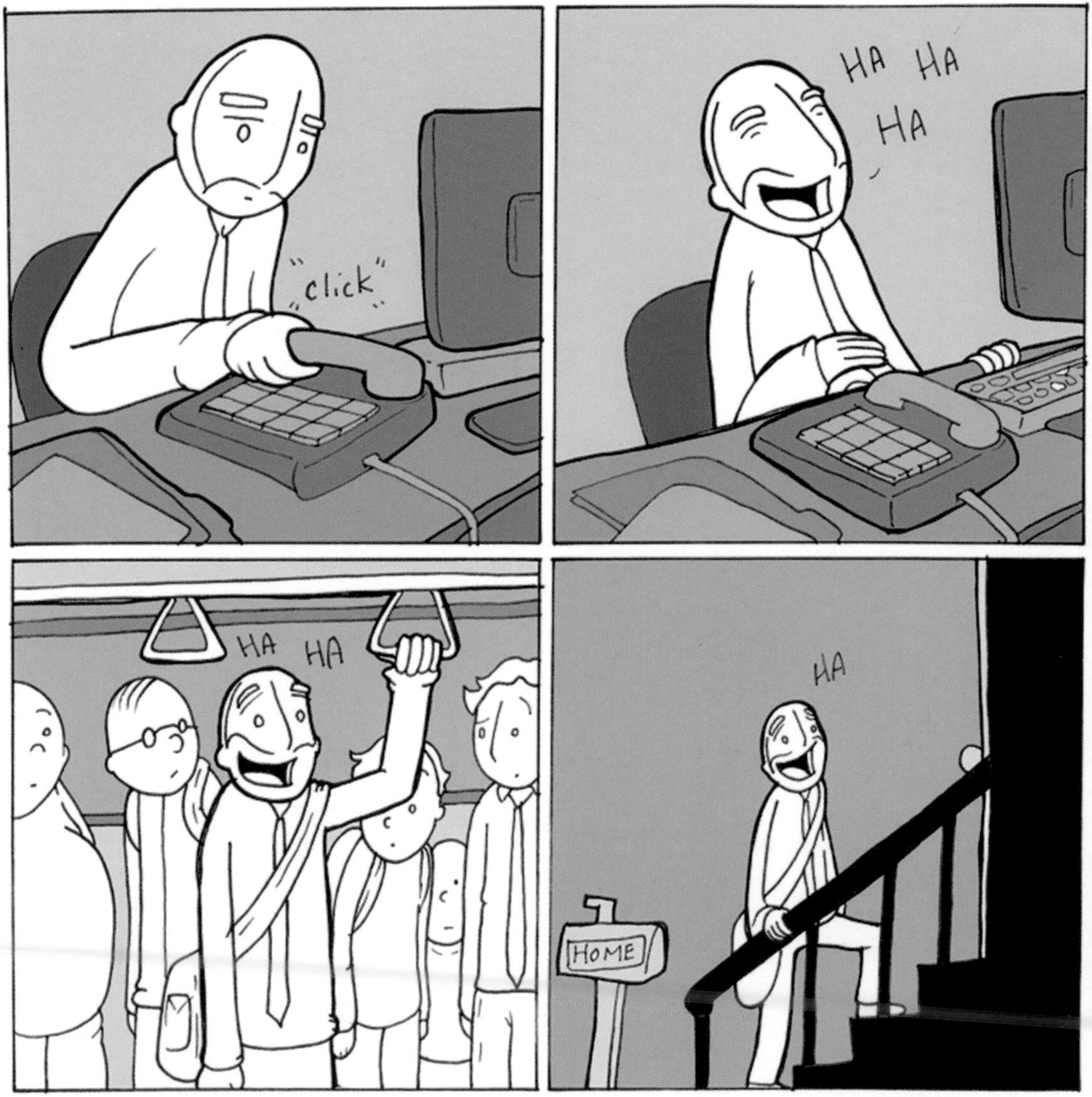
"click"
HA HA
HA
HA HA
HA
HOME

91

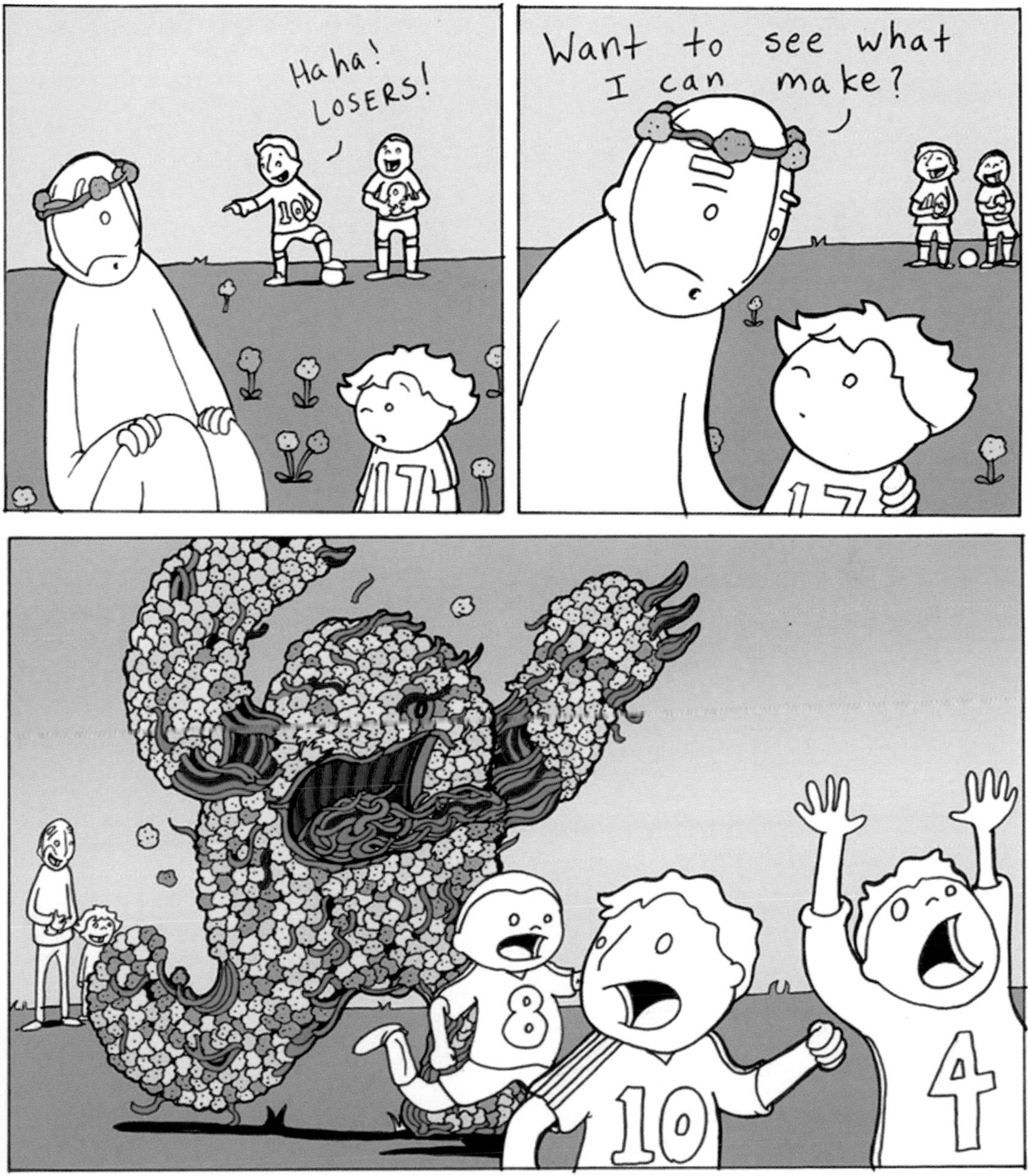
Haha! LOSERS!
Want to see what I can make?

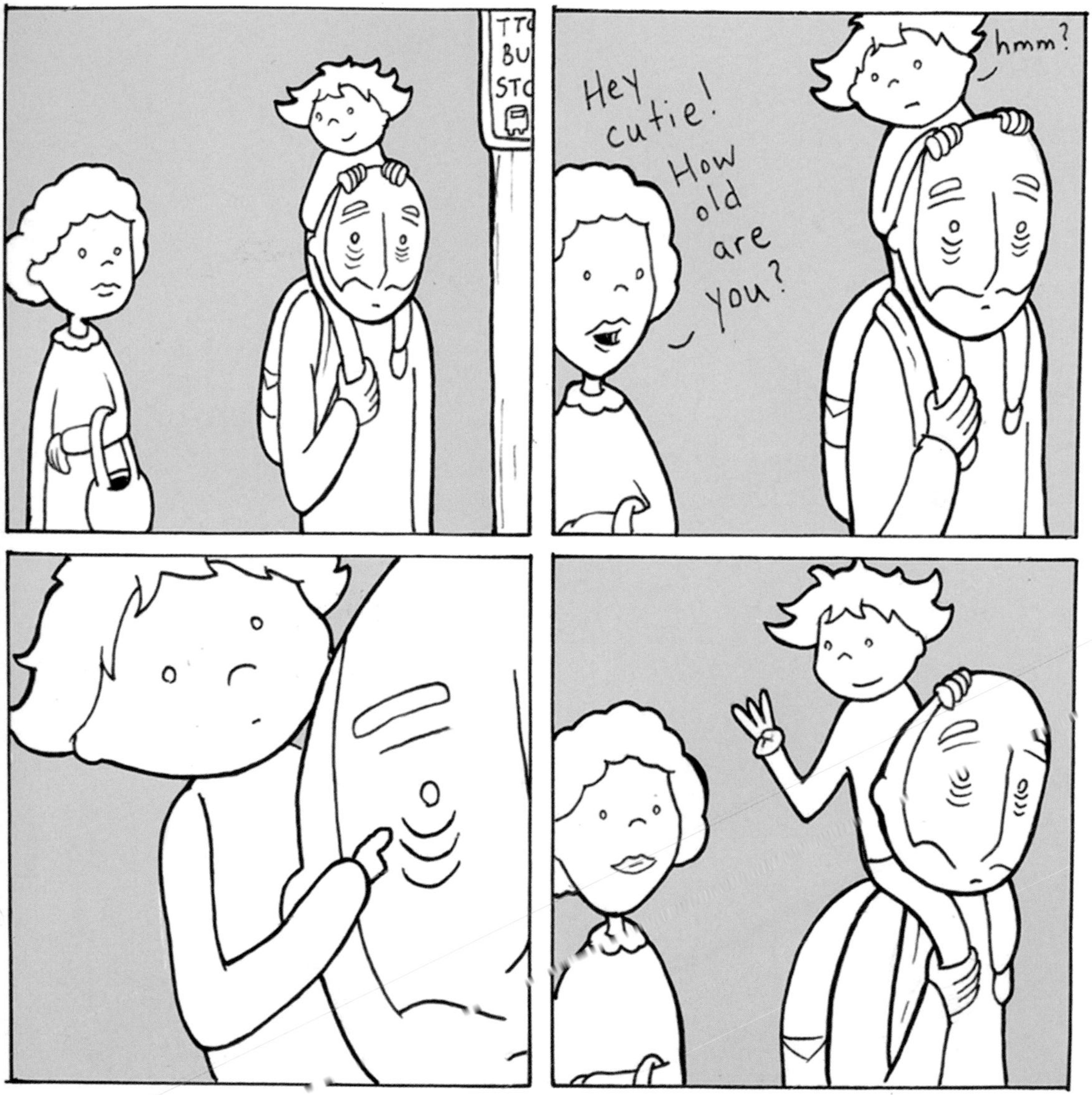
TTC BUS STOP
Hey cutie! How old are you?
hmm?

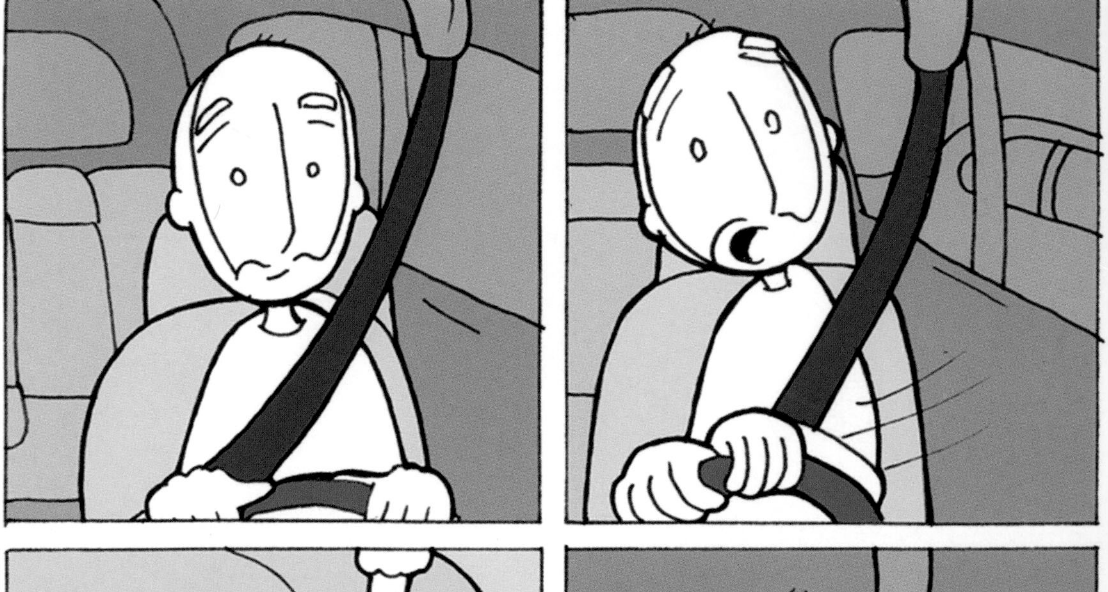
Stupid
Fucking
Asshole!
dick
head

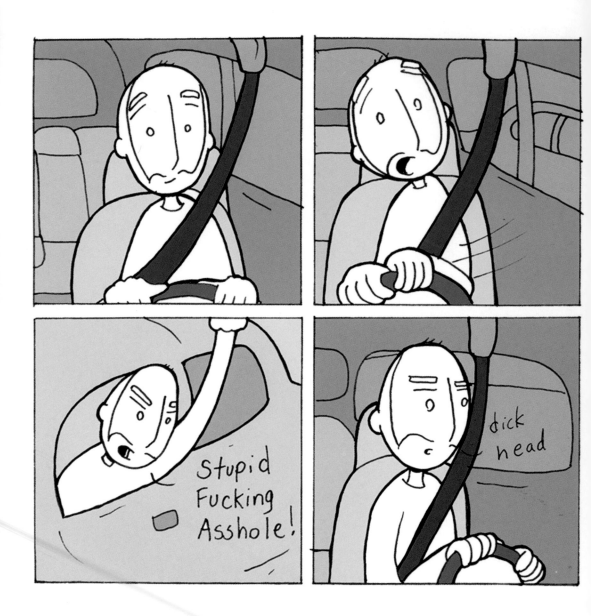

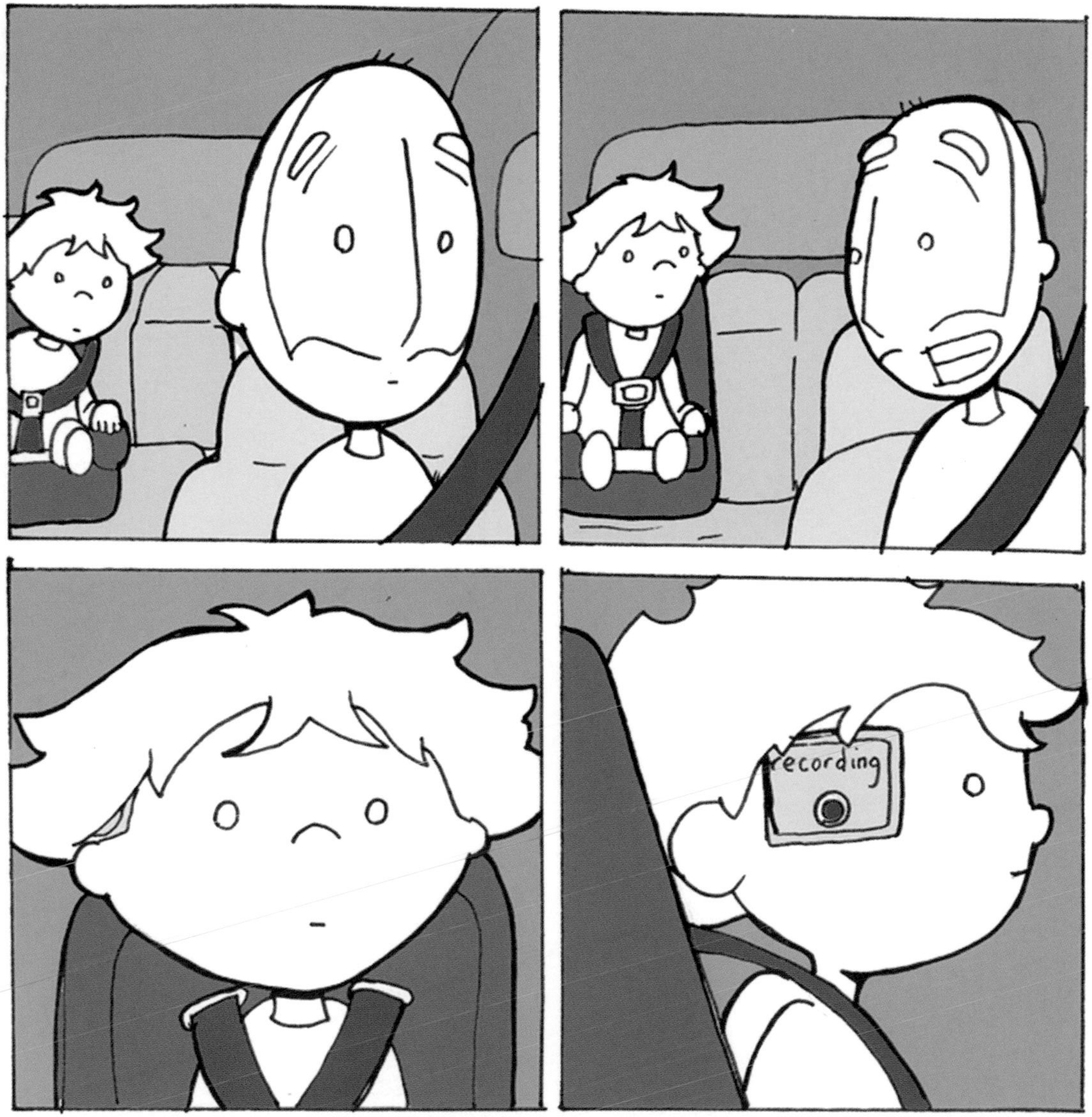
recording

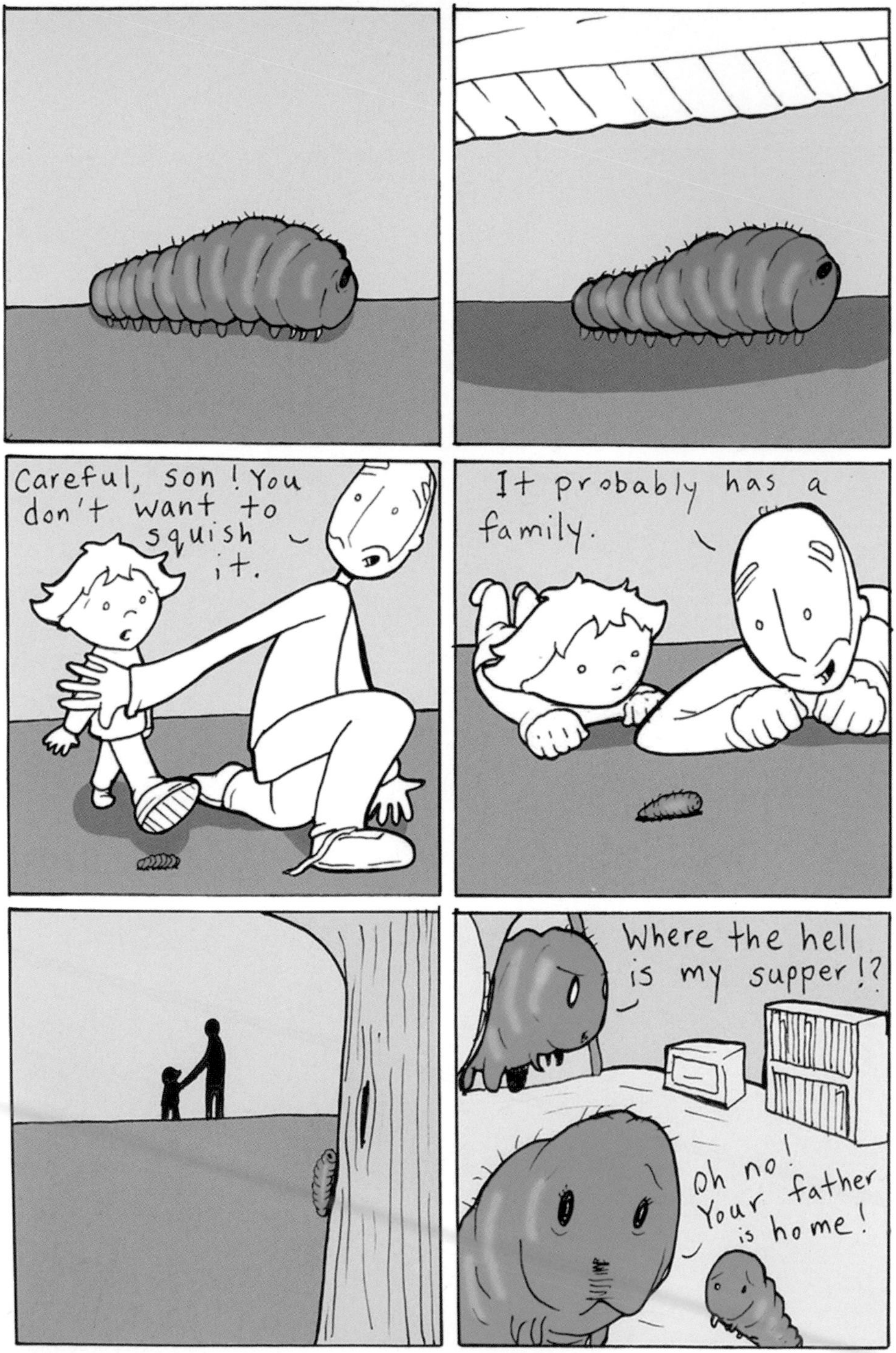
Careful, son! You don't want to squish it.
It probably has a family.
Where the hell is my supper!?
Oh no! Your father is home!

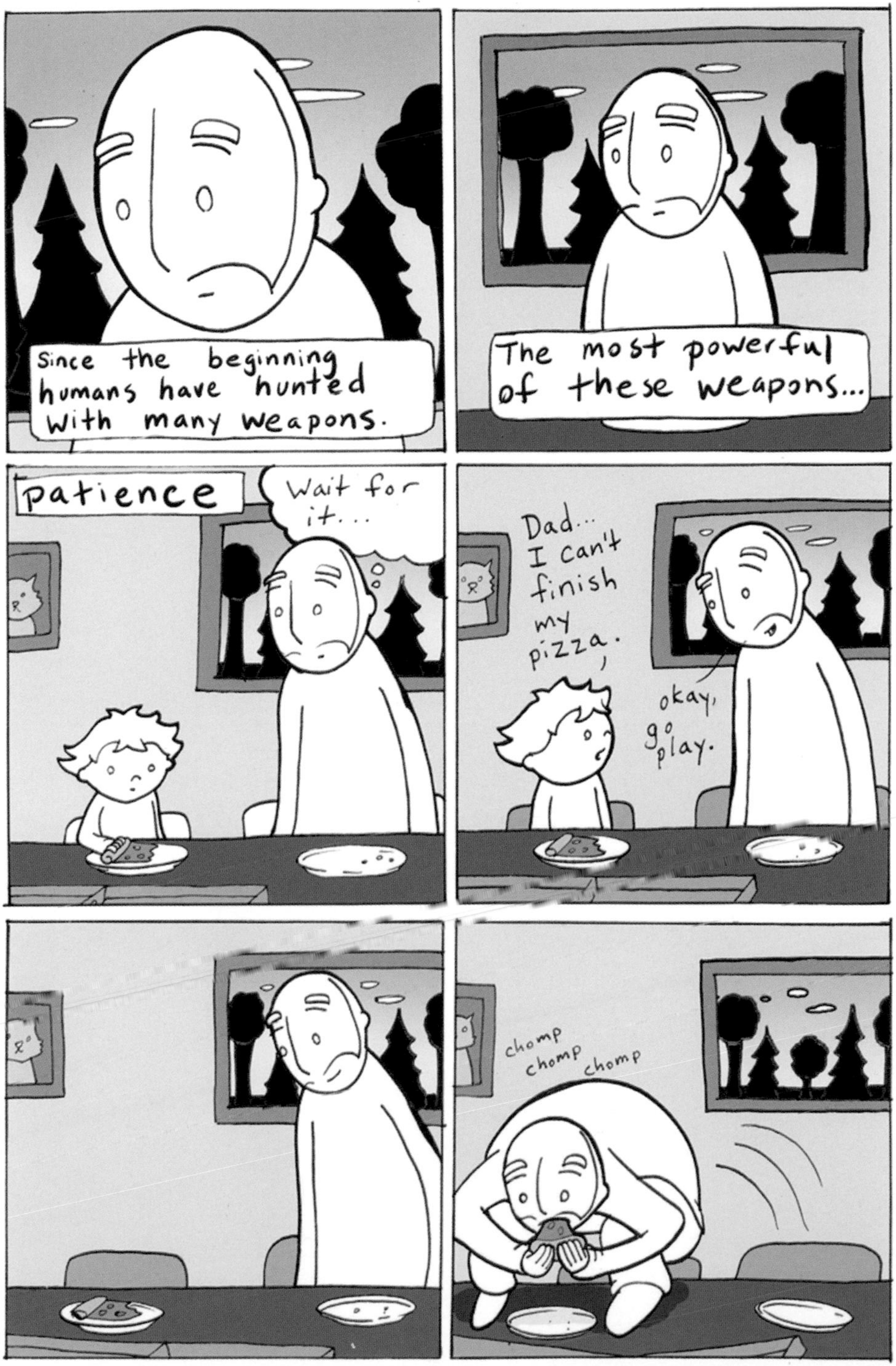
Since the beginning humans have hunted with many weapons.
The most powerful of these weapons...
patience
Wait for it...
Dad... I can't finish my pizza.
okay, go play.
chomp chomp chomp

100

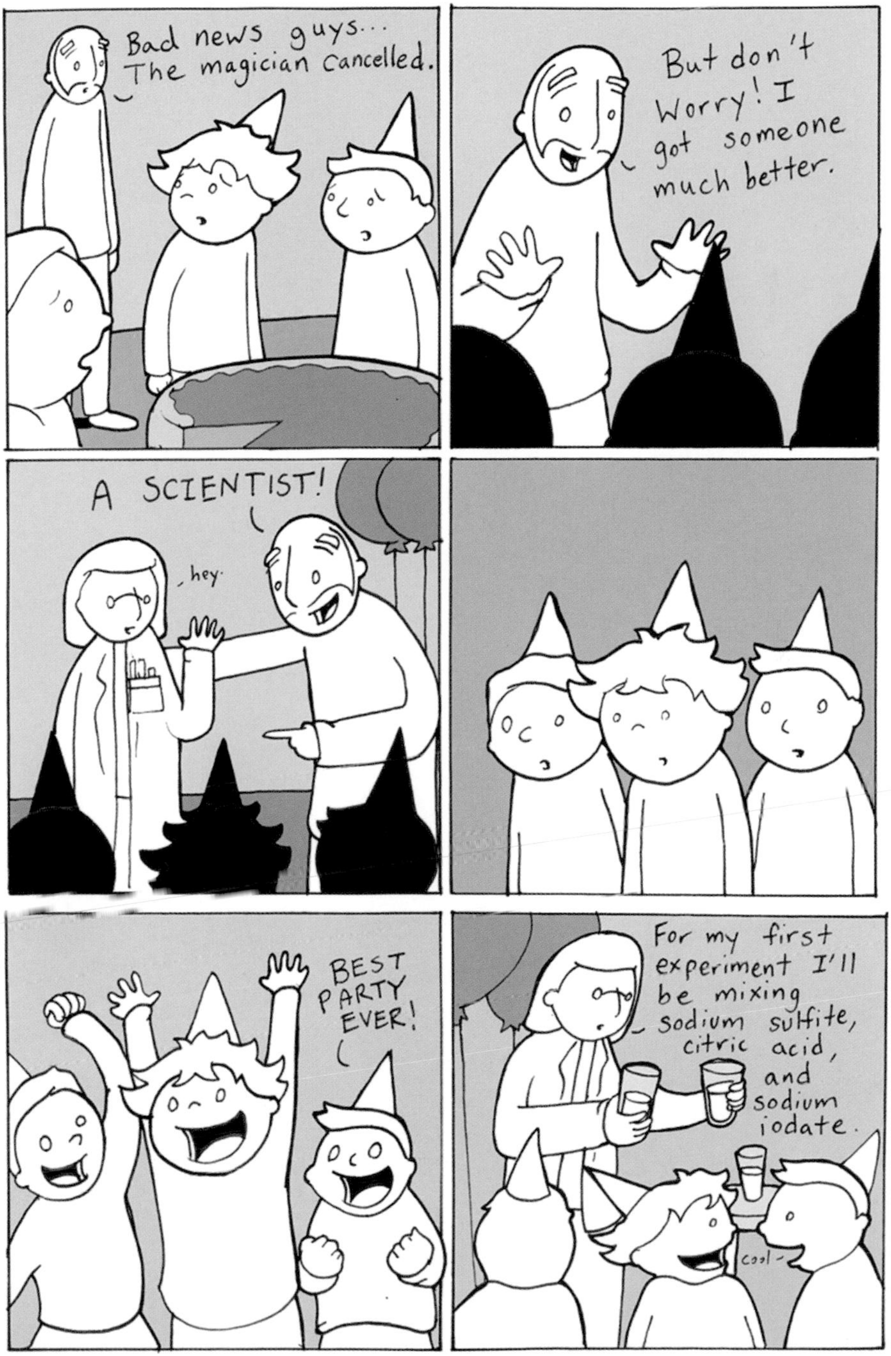
Bad news guys...
The magician cancelled.
But don't worry! I got someone much better.
A SCIENTIST!
hey.
BEST PARTY EVER!
For my first experiment I'll be mixing sodium sulfite, citric acid, and sodium iodate.
cool

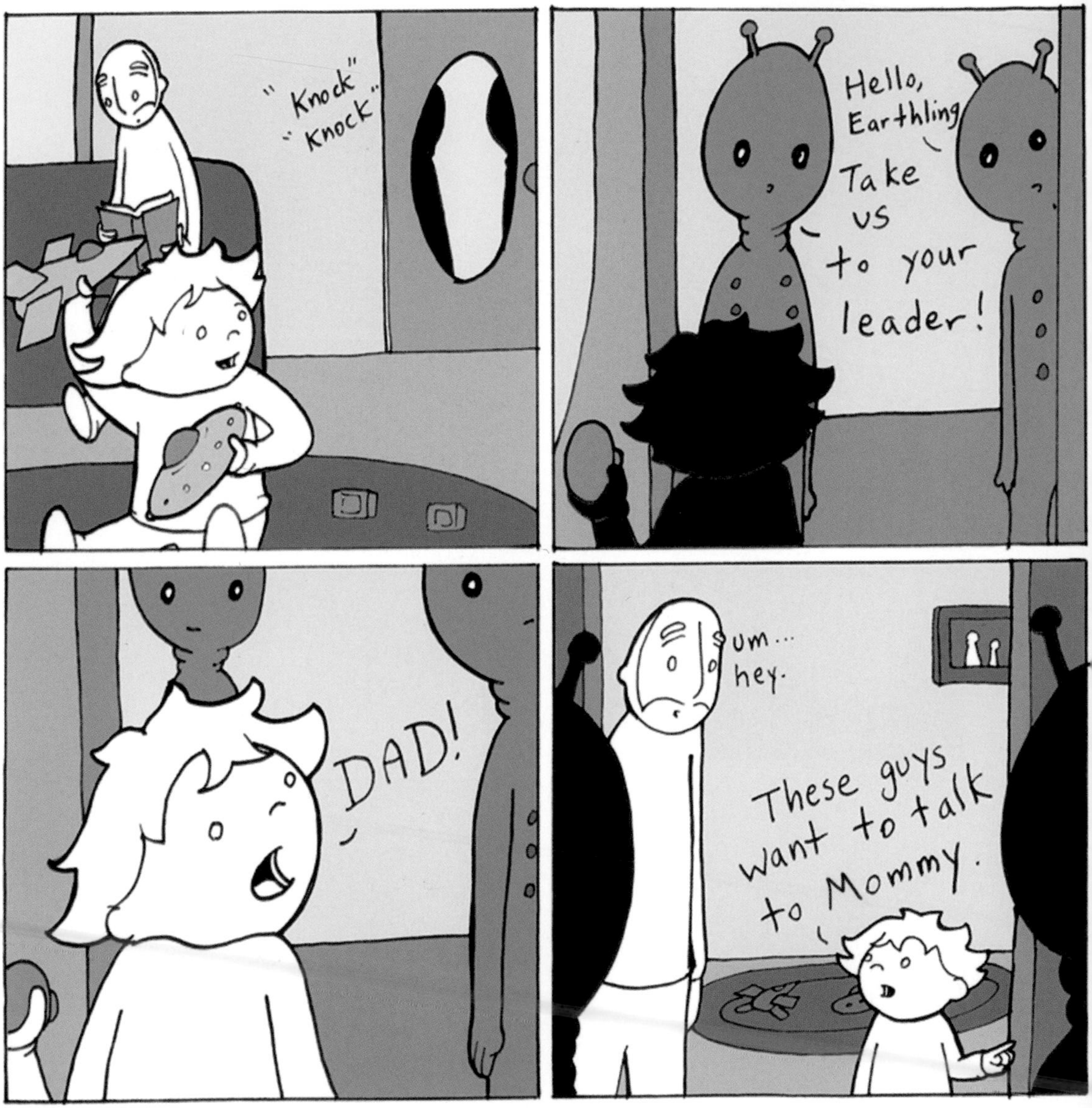
"Knock"
"Knock"
Hello, Earthling
Take us to your leader!
DAD!
um... hey.
These guys want to talk to Mommy.

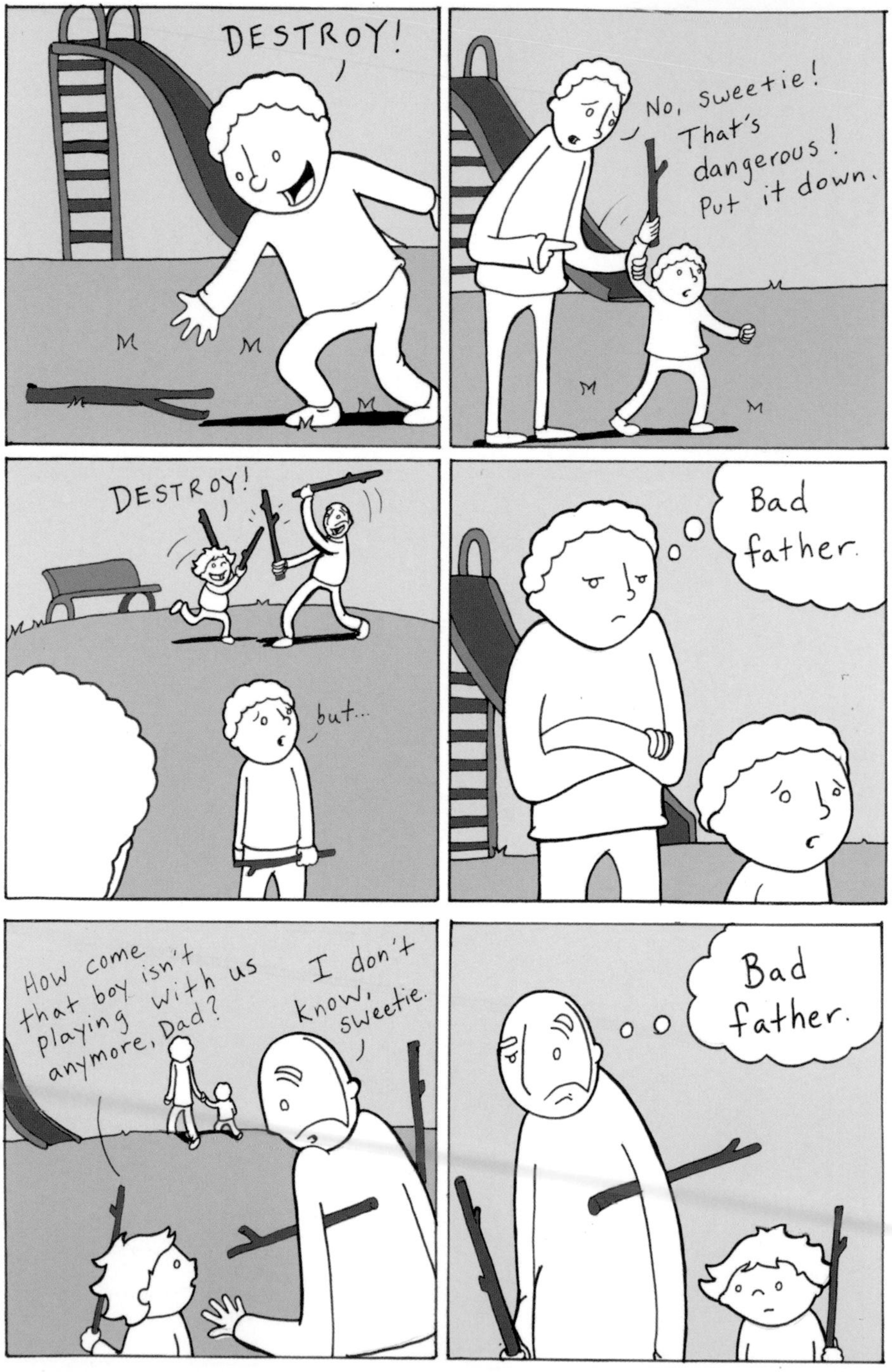
DESTROY!
No, sweetie! That's dangerous! Put it down.
DESTROY!
but...
Bad father.
How come that boy isn't playing with us anymore, Dad?
I don't know, sweetie.
Bad father.

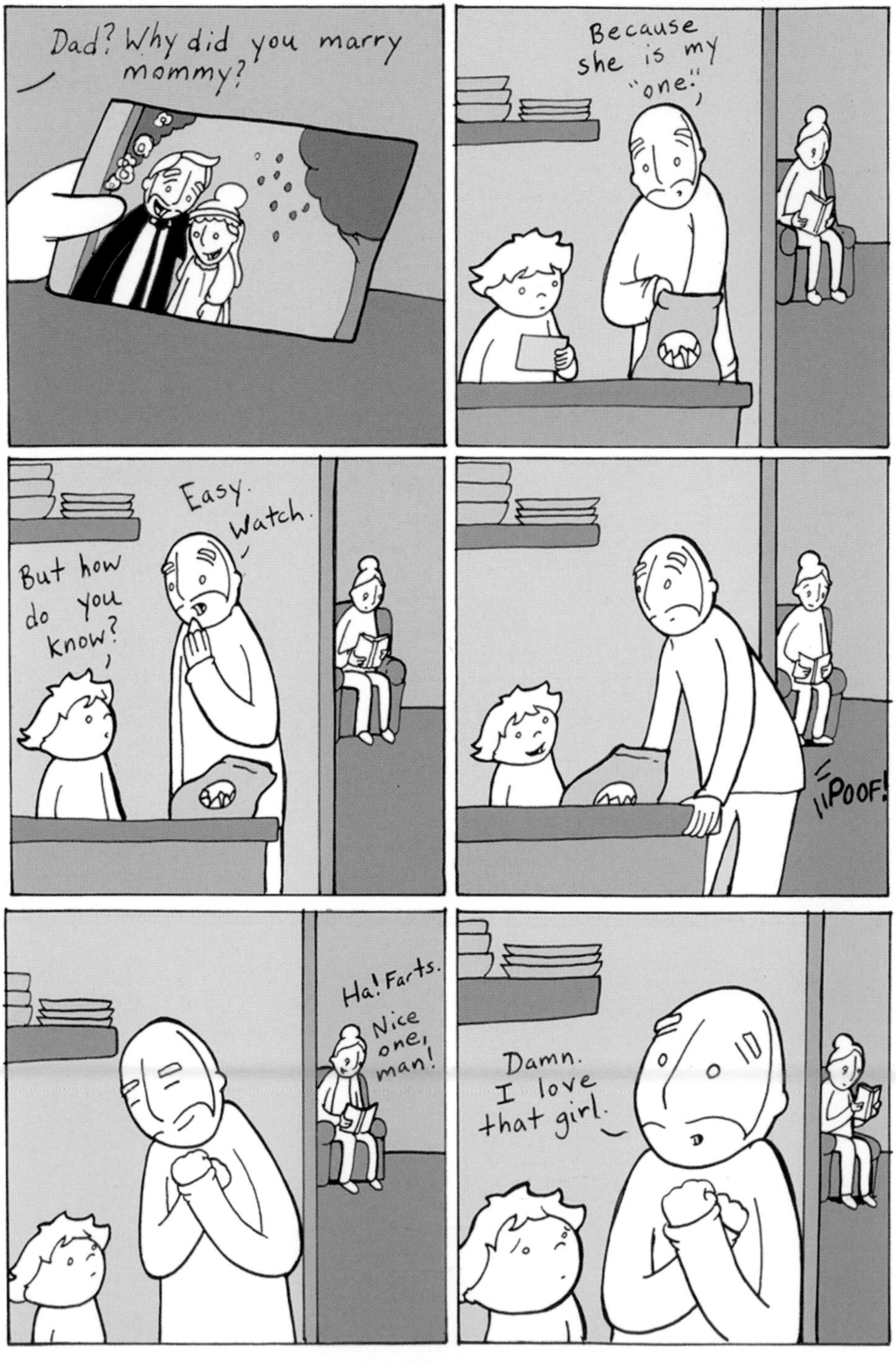
Dad? Why did you marry mommy?
Because she is my "one."
But how do you know?
Easy. Watch.
POOF!
Ha! Farts.
Nice one, man!
Damn. I love that girl.

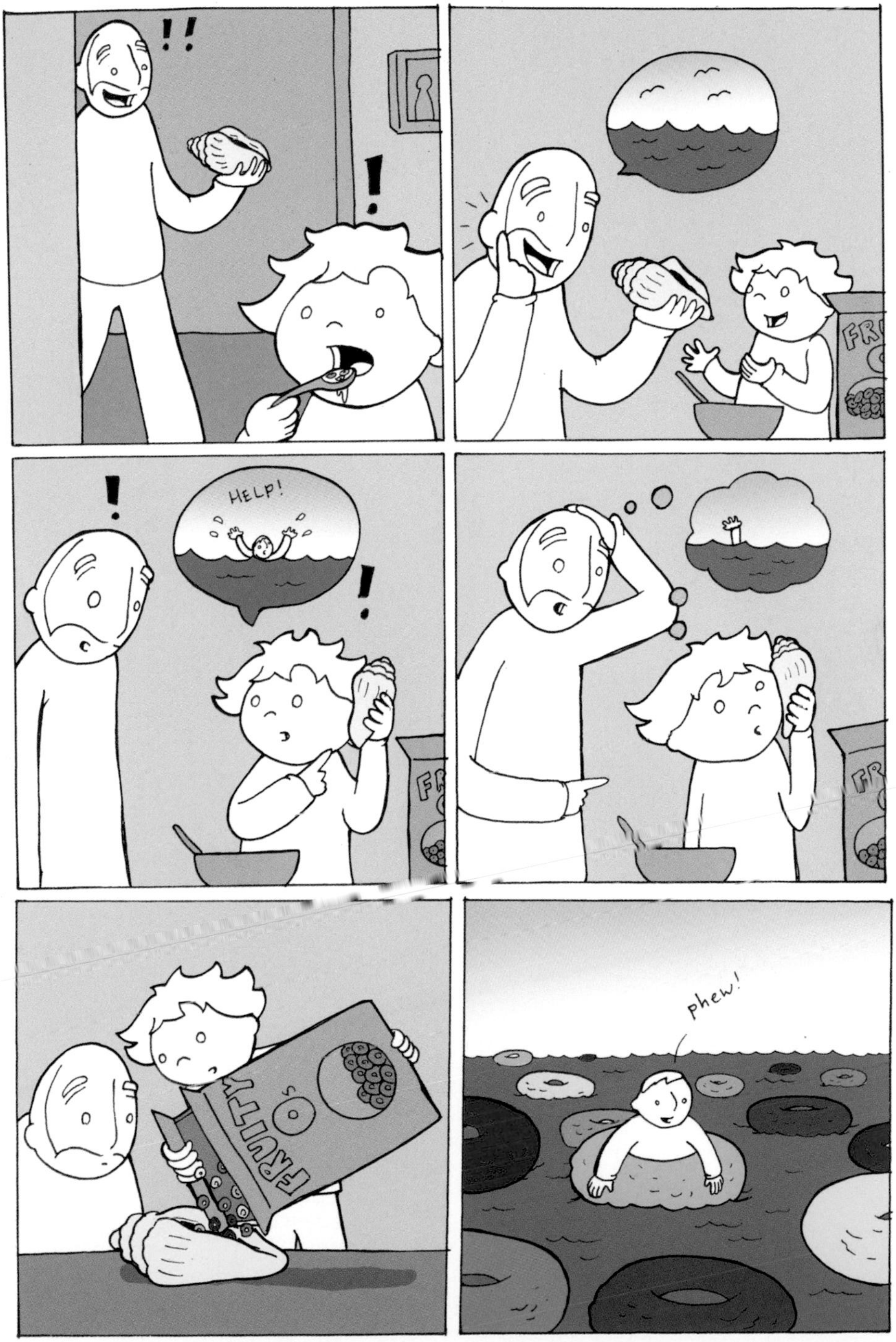
!!
!
HELP!
!
!
FRUITY O's
phew!

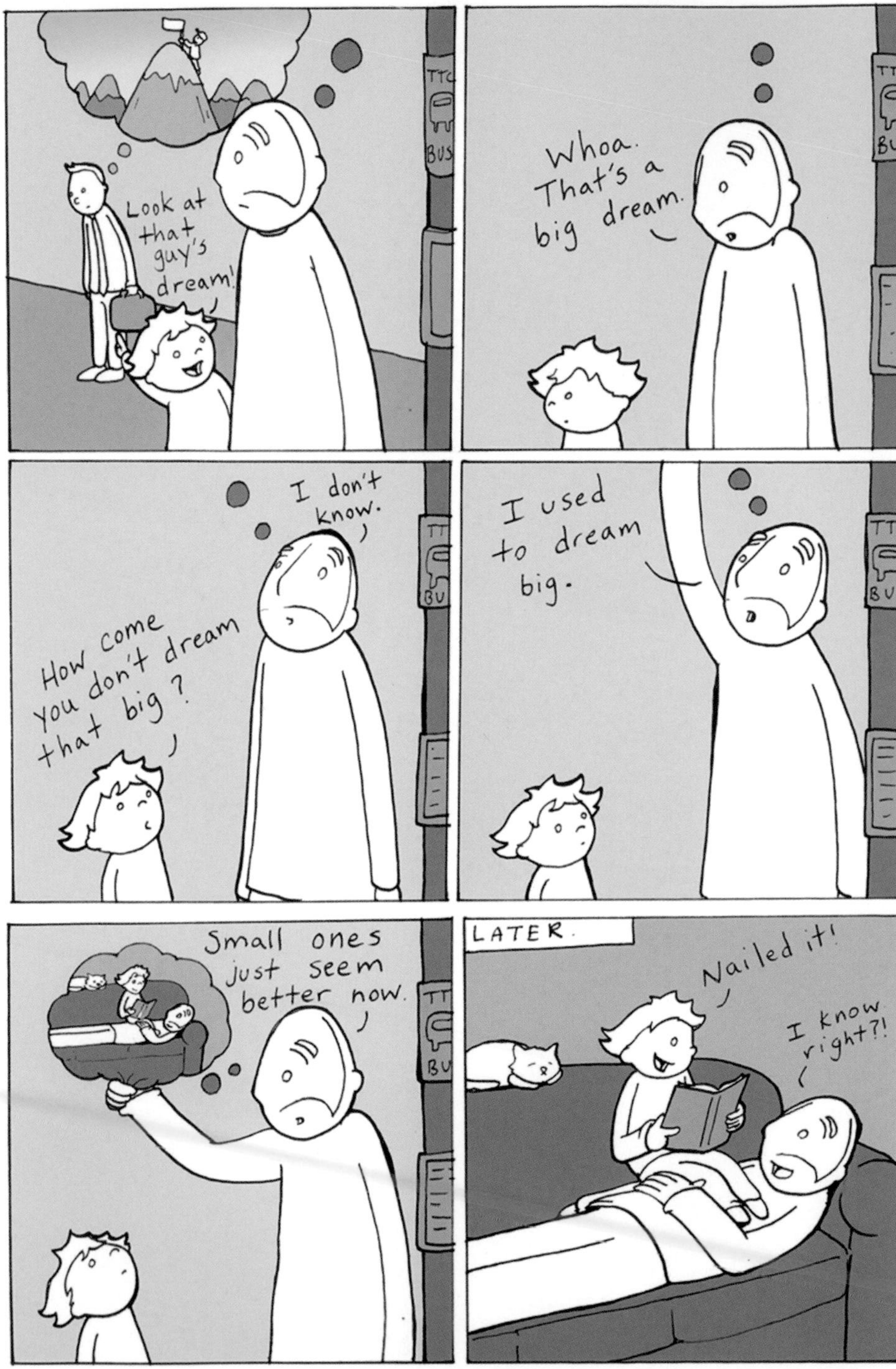
Look at that guy's dream!
Whoa. That's a big dream.
How come you don't dream that big?
I don't know.
I used to dream big.
Small ones just seem better now.
LATER.
Nailed it!
I know right?!
TTC
BUS

109

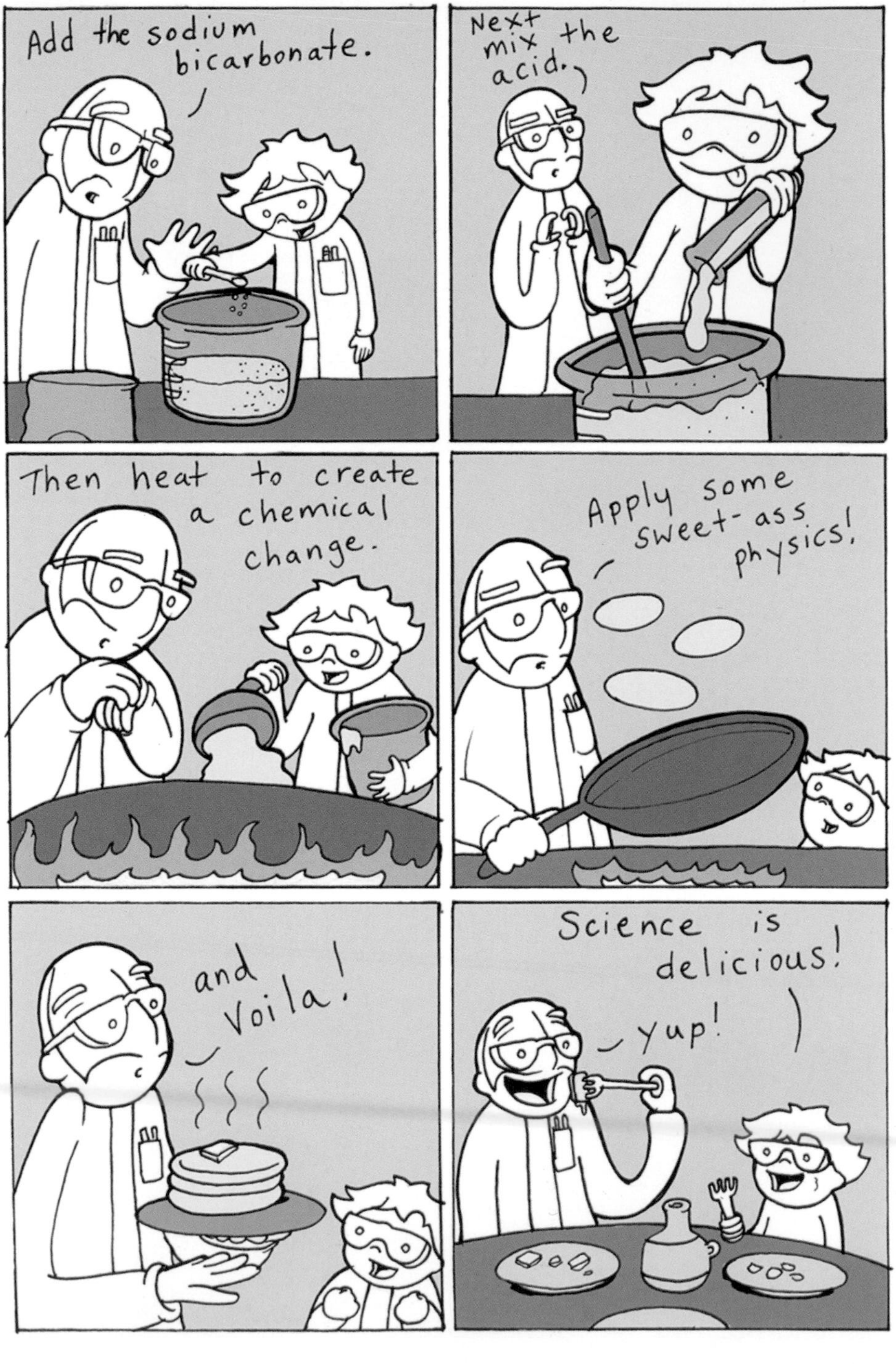
Add the sodium bicarbonate.
Next mix the acid.
Then heat to create a chemical change.
Apply some sweet-ass physics!
and Voila!
Science is delicious!
yup!

112

114

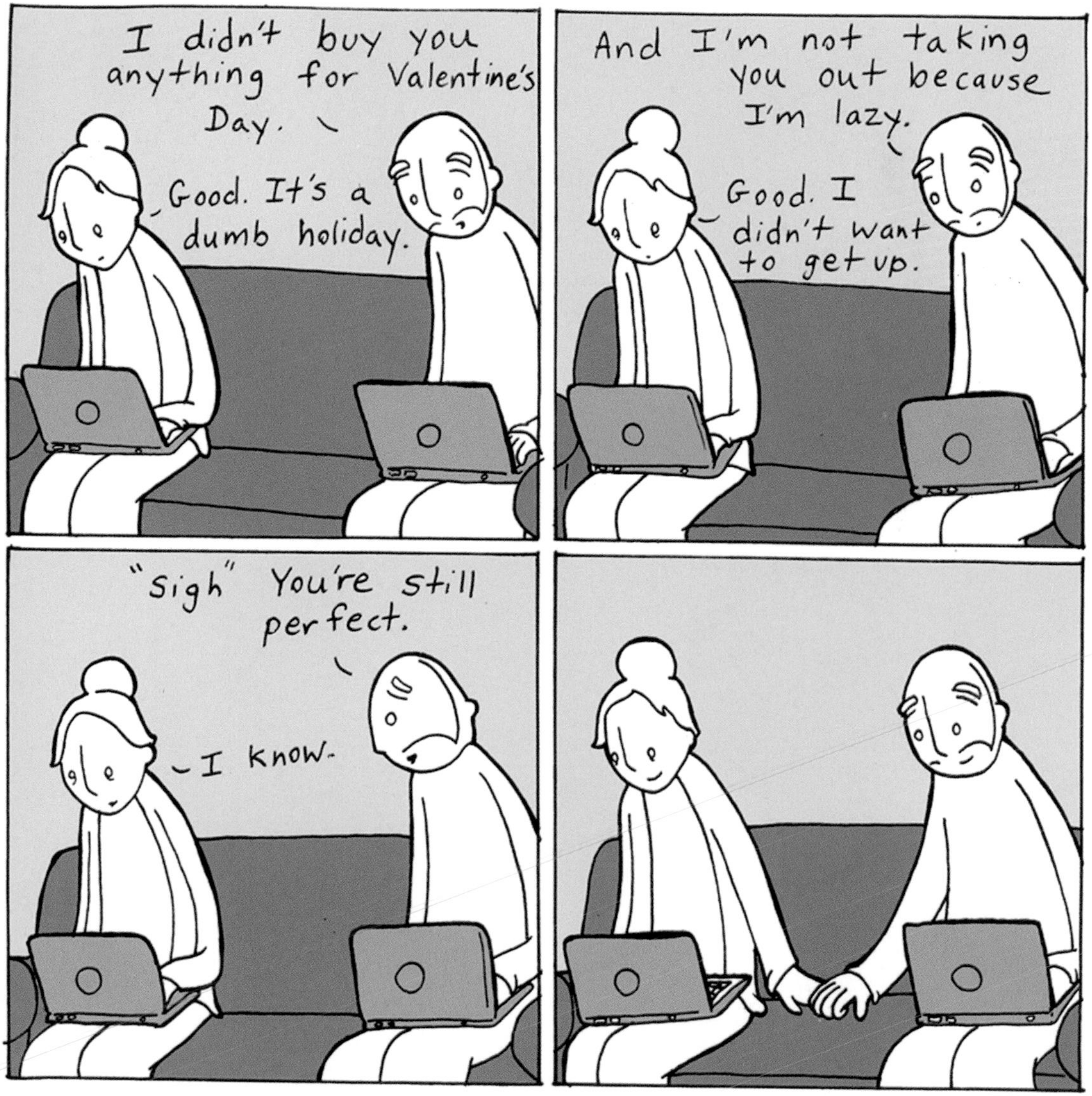
I didn't buy you anything for Valentine's Day.
Good. It's a dumb holiday.
And I'm not taking you out because I'm lazy.
Good. I didn't want to get up.
"sigh" You're still perfect.
I know.

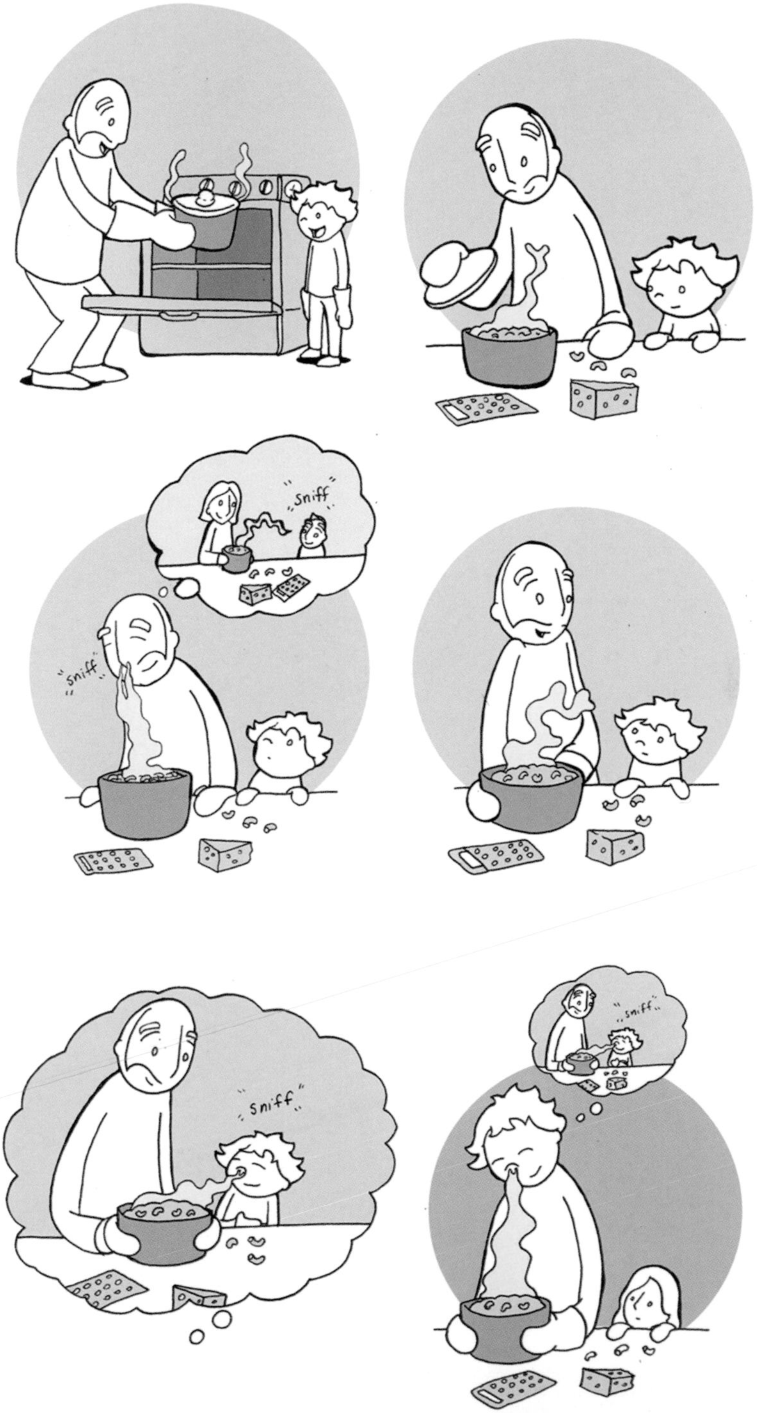
sniff
sniff
sniff
sniff

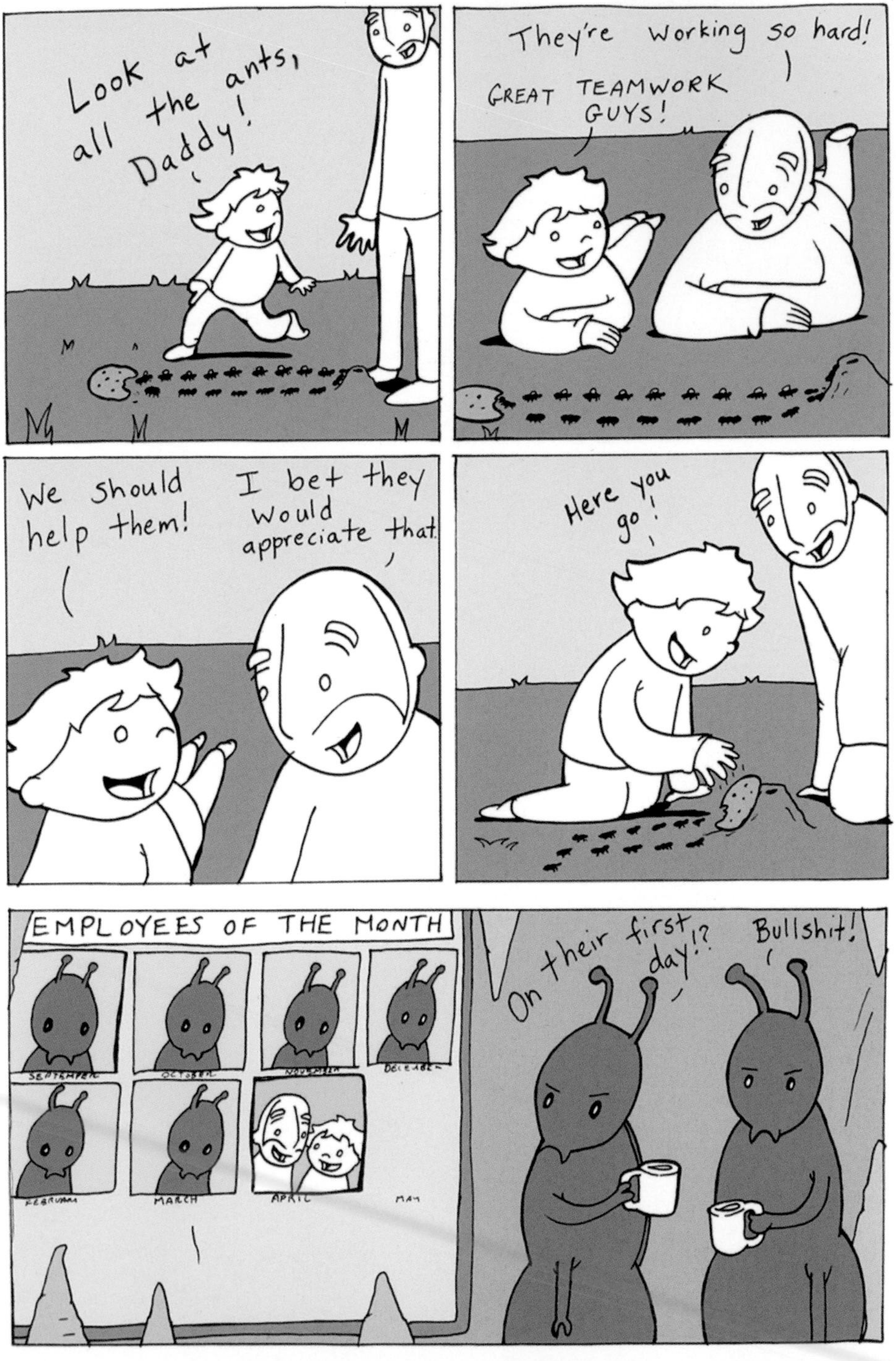

Look at all the ants, Daddy!
They're working so hard!
GREAT TEAMWORK GUYS!
We should help them!
I bet they would appreciate that.
Here you go!
EMPLOYEES OF THE MONTH
MARCH
APRIL
On their first day!?
Bullshit!

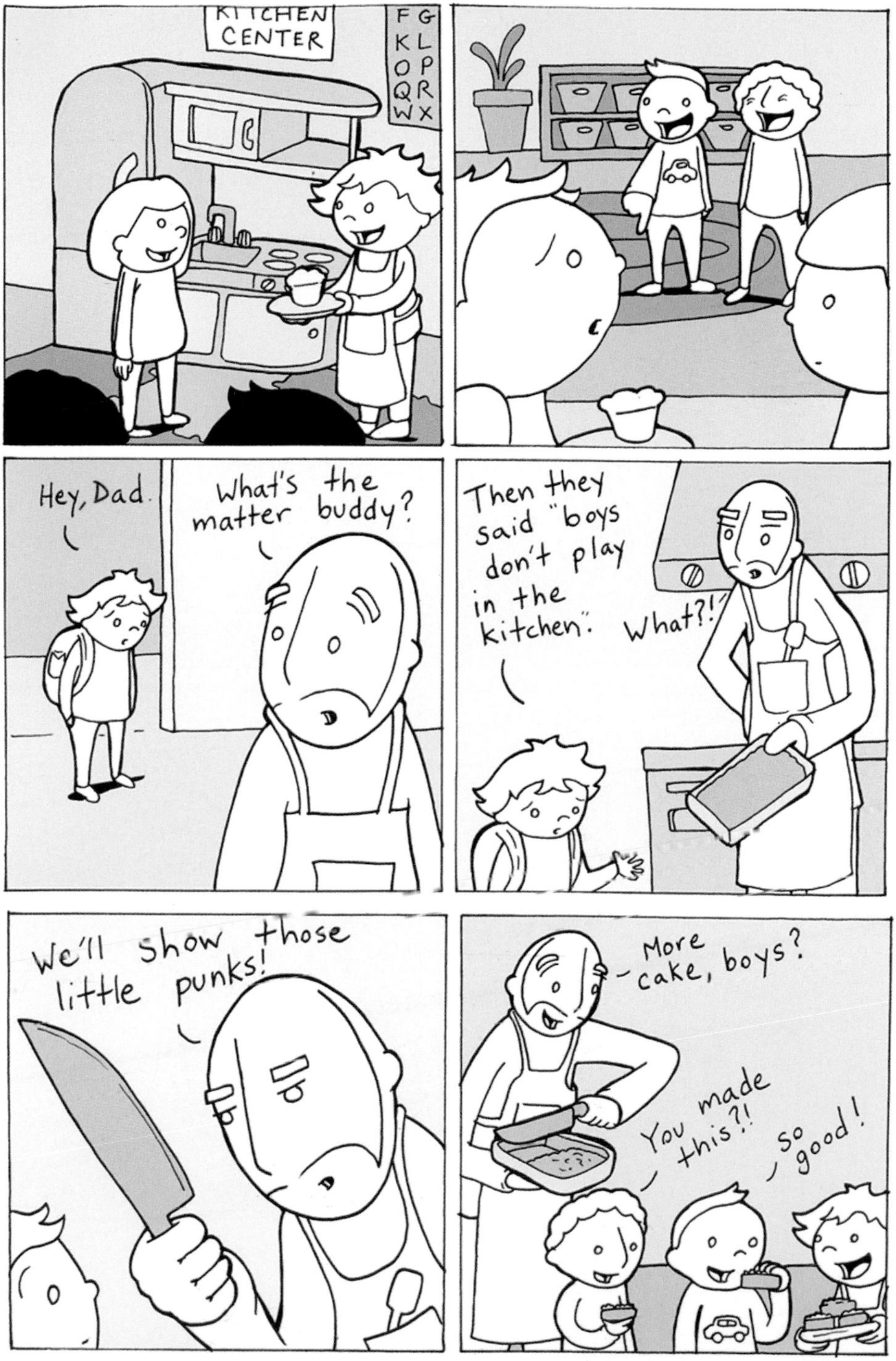
KITCHEN CENTER
F G K L O P Q R W X
Hey, Dad.
What's the matter buddy?
Then they said "boys don't play in the kitchen."
What?!
We'll show those little punks!
More cake, boys?
You made this?!
So good!

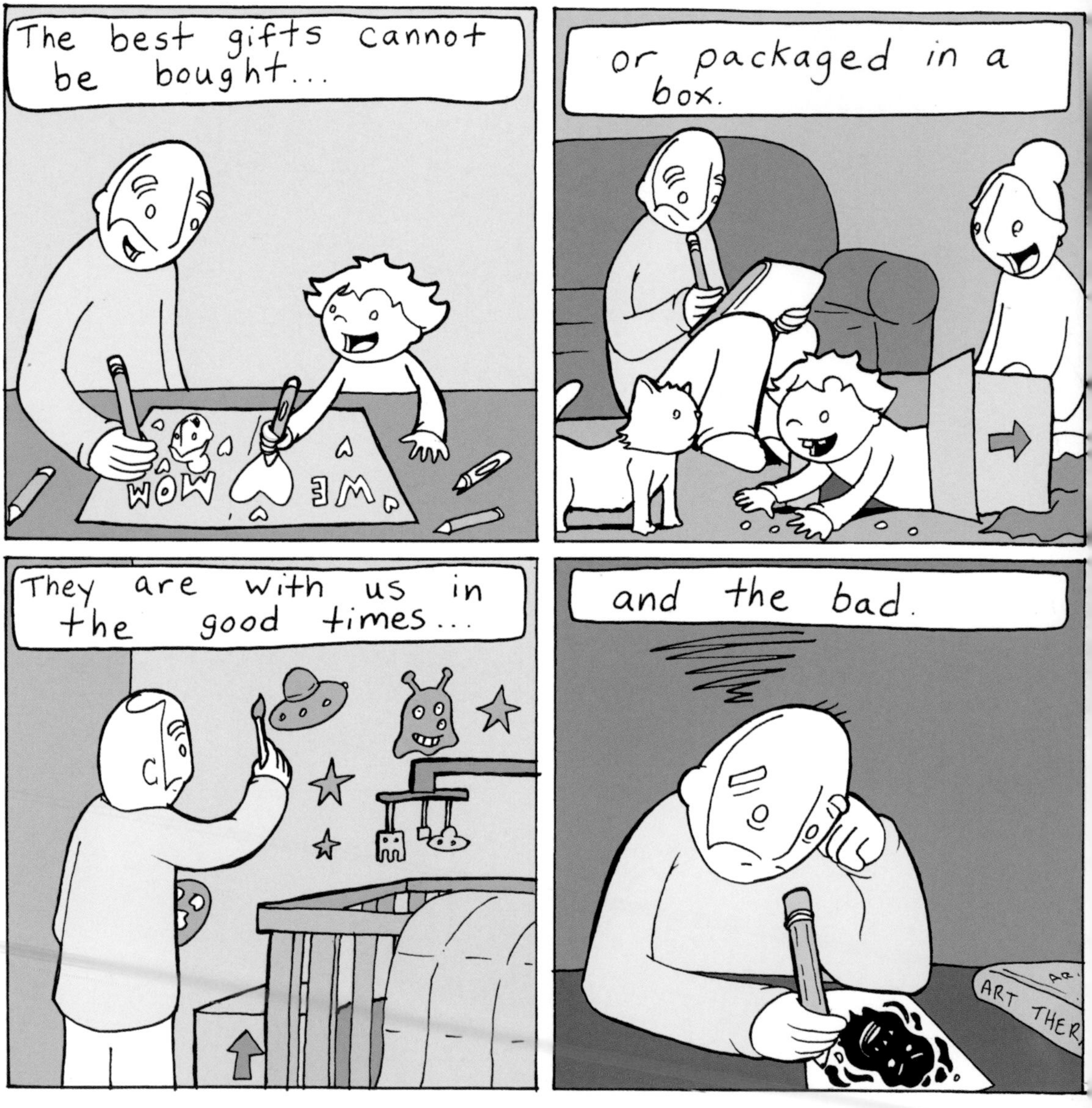
The best gifts cannot be bought...
WE
MOM
or packaged in a box.
They are with us in the good times...
and the bad.
ART THER

The best gifts stay with us forever.

They make us who we are.

And no matter how many times we say "thank you"...

It will never be enough.

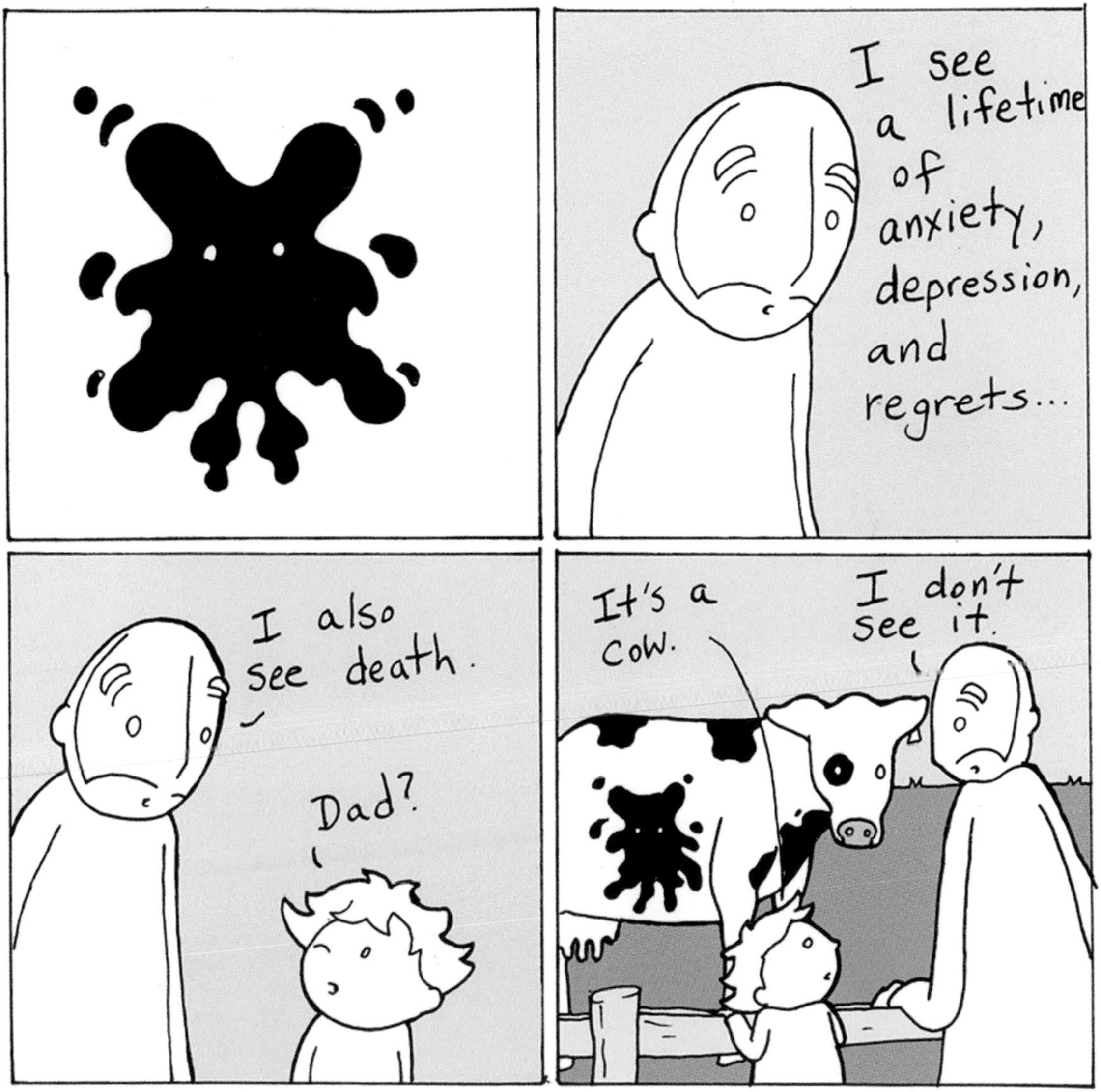
I see a lifetime of anxiety, depression, and regrets...
I also see death.
Dad?
It's a cow.
I don't see it.

125

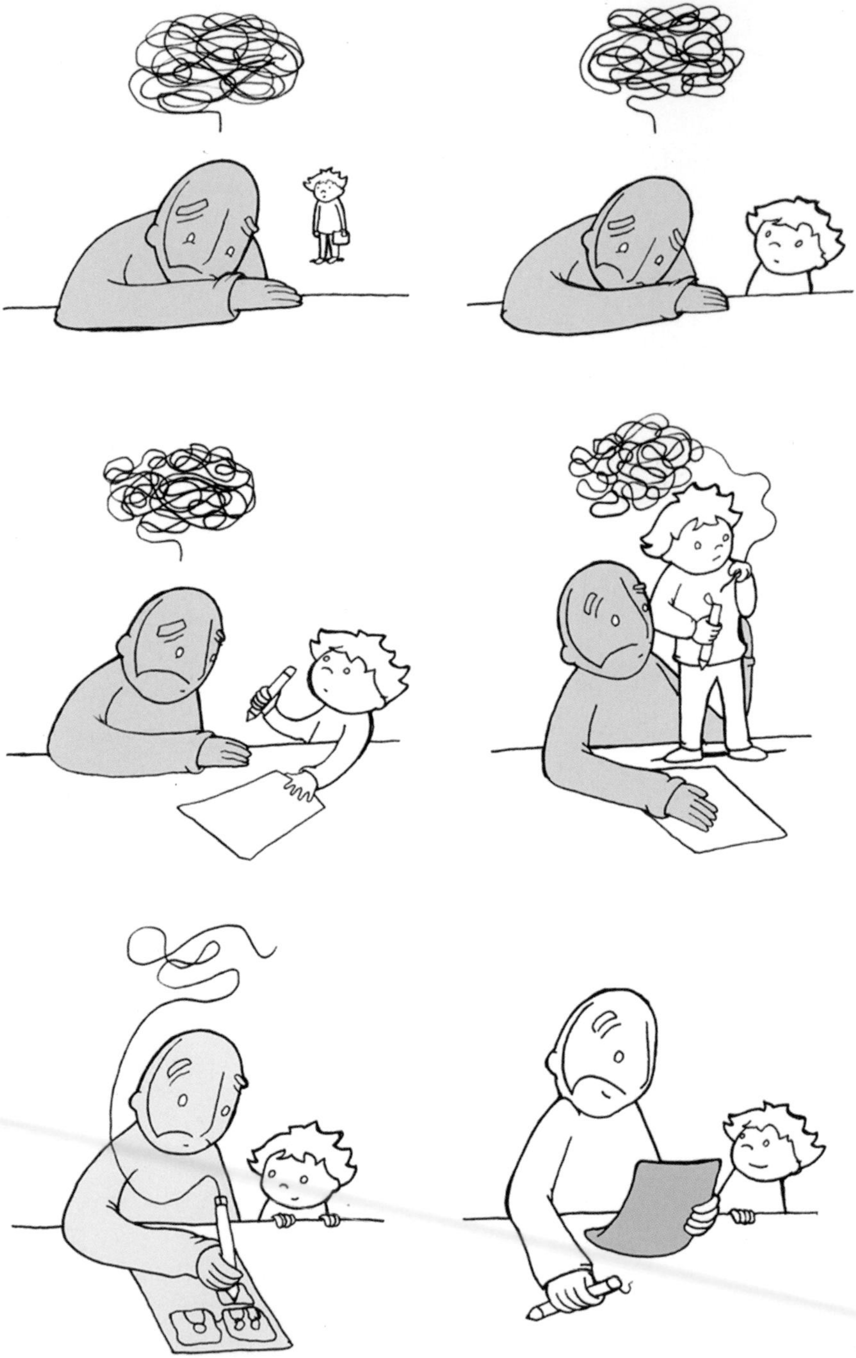